W9-BJC-435

THE ARTFUL EDIT

ON THE PRACTICE OF EDITING YOURSELF

THE
ARTFUL EDIT
ON THE PRACTICE OF EDITING YOURSELF

SUSAN BELL

W. W. Norton & Company
New York London

For information about permission to reproduce selections from this book, write to Permissions, W. W. Norton & Company, Inc. 500 Fifth Avenue, New York, NY 10110

For information about special discounts for bulk purchases, please contact W. W. Norton Special Sales at specialsales@wwnorton.com or 800-233-4830.

Manufacturing by Quebecor Fairfield
Book design by Rhea Braunstein
Production manager: Julia Druskin

Library of Congress Cataloging-in-Publication Data

Bell, Susan (Susan P.), 1958–
The artful edit : on the practice of editing yourself / Susan Bell. — 1st ed.
    p. cm.
  Includes bibliographical references.
  ISBN 978-0-393-05752-2 (hardcover)
1. Editing. I. Title.
PN162.B44 2007
808'.027—dc22

                                                              2007013513

W. W. Norton & Company, Inc.
500 Fifth Avenue, New York, N.Y. 10110
www.wwnorton.com

W. W. Norton & Company Ltd.
Castle House, 75/76 Wells Street,
London W1T 3QT

1 2 3 4 5 6 7 8 9 0

For Lucia

We're grafting these branches onto a tree that already had an organic, balanced structure. Knowing that we're changing the organism, we're trying not to do anything toxic to it, and to keep everything in some kind of balance. At this point, I don't know what the result will be. I have some intuitions, but my mind is completely open.

Walter Murch

The friends that have it I do wrong
When ever I remake a song,
Should know what issue is at stake:
It is myself that I remake.

William Butler Yeats

CONTENTS

Note on gender:

To be inclusive, yet avoid the ungraceful conjunctions of "he/she" and "he or she," this book alternates male and female pronouns, chapter by chapter. In the introduction, both pronouns are used.

SB

INTRODUCTION

I have no right to expect others to do for me what
I should do for myself.

Thomas Wolfe

Many writers hanker to learn about a process that lives at a hushed remove from the "glamour" of writing: the edit. They want what most creative-writing classrooms are hard-pressed to give, which is detachment from their text in order to see it clearly. Students are generally taught to rely on others to see it on their behalf, and risk creating a dubious dependency. Classroom critiques, while helpful, are limited. Too often they don't give a systematic view of a writer's work, and train him to develop a thick skin more than a sensible one.

In 2001, New York's New School graduate writing program invited me to teach a course in self-editing, based on my belief that writing improves dramatically when, at the draft stage, a writer learns to think and act like an editor. The debate continues on whether you can teach someone to write; I know, unequivocally, that you can teach someone to edit. For twenty years, I have edited writers and at the same time coached them to read themselves more closely; with every new project, they need me less because they have learned to edit themselves better.

All writers—restrained or lyrical, avant-garde or traditional, avocational or professional—need to revise, yet editing is commonly taught as an intrinsic part of writing, not an external tool. As such, the practice is elusive and random; it induces panicky flailing more than discipline and patience. It is vital to teach editing on its own terms, not as a shadowy aspect of writing. Writers need to learn to calibrate editing's singular blend of mechanics and magic. For if writing builds the house, nothing but revision will complete it. One writer needs to be two carpenters: a builder with mettle, and a finisher with slow hands.

Writers live with many fears—of success, of failure, of a ten-year project garnering a one-year paycheck. Their greatest fear, however, is of their own intimate voice, and they find many ways to subvert hearing it. Before she takes up the nuts and bolts of revision, a writer must face the metaphysical challenge of gaining perspective on her own words. Let's reflect on the kind of inspiration that may fuel a writer: wrenching memories, transgressive desires, politically incorrect conceits, bad jokes, and other aesthetic faux pas. These constitute that painfully intimate voice she would rather avoid. We are loath to put an objective ear to our subjective selves. But *to edit is to listen*, above all; to hear past the emotional filters that distort the sound of our all too human words; and to then make choices rather than judgments. As we read our writing, how can we learn to hear ourselves better?

The purpose of *The Artful Edit* is not to devise a set editorial regimen, but to discuss the myriad possibilities of the drafted page and help you acquire the editorial consciousness needed to direct them. There are concrete methods here to aid this mission. One sure method for learning to edit yourself, for example, is to edit others (which you'll be encouraged to do in the section on partner edits in chapter three). The point is to implant the conversation between editor and writer into the writer's head; so that, when the time comes, the writer can split into two and treat herself as a good editor would. Editing others not only deepens your understanding of text, but trains your mind to look dispassionately and pragmatically at a work, even your own.

⌣

To learn the widest spectrum of editorial options, history matters. *The Artful Edit* tries to understand how the species *Homo editus* has evolved over time, and how it now lives in the twenty-first century. Where, in fact, do editors come from? How did editors in nineteenth-century France discuss a writer's work with him? How do American editors do so now, at the beginning of the twenty-first century? Most literature, since the late 1400s, has been altered by the editorial process on its way to the public. With the advent of the printing press to fifteenth-century Venice, medieval scribes gave way to textual critics (literary detectives hired by publishers to authenticate manuscripts); and along the way, the modern editor, who works with living authors, was born. He would migrate to American soil, some four centuries later, where he would flourish.

The editor's viewpoint has affected, in small or large part, almost all texts over time. Some works have incurred only a change in punctuation. Others were tossed into the editor's sieve, until the chunky parts of speech were removed and the fine, smooth powder of an idea remained. Still others were aided by editorial consultation that yielded new concepts and directions.

Editor Gordon Lish assisted Raymond Carver in the minutiae of sentence making, while F. Scott Fitzgerald received story ideas, not line edits, from his editor, Maxwell Perkins. Against a historical backdrop, we will assimilate the true meaning and scope of the word "edit." History will help us see editing as an independent craft, and editors—including writers who edit themselves—as true craftsmen.

Some writers are downright suspicious of editors. It is true: Shakespeare had no editor and, well, he wrote just fine. But at the risk of stating the obvious, we do not all possess Shakespeare's gifts. Besides, Shakespeare penned his immortal lines in the relative quiet of sixteenth-century Britain, untempted by iPods and mobile phones. The blinding pace and complexity of the modern world may just keep writers from literally seeing all they need to in their manuscripts. Take computers. Nearly every author in the Western world, and a good many beyond, uses a computer—a device that makes the editorial enterprise both more appealing and more troublesome. People tend to think the computer is the supreme editing tool. Sure, editing on a computer is easy to do *physically*. But that gloriously easy machinery may well soften the editorial muscle *mentally*. For Gerald Howard, executive editor at Doubleday, "word processors have made the physical act of producing a novel so much easier that you can see manuscripts that have word processoritis. They're swollen and [the writing] looks so good, arranged in such an attractive format that how could it not be good? Well, it's NOT good, and there's too much of it!" When a writer had to deal with the laborious task of pounding out seventy-five or a hundred thousand words on a manual typewriter, Howard went on, he would "be a lot more careful about the sentences he allowed to get into manuscript form."

Introduction

Most of us who write on computers are facing and continually accessing a global Internet lodged in our writing instrument. Shakespeare's world was neither small nor simple, but he didn't have to face nearly every aspect of it on the web, nor a full inbox of personal and junk mail, each time he set to write. A pen was, after all, just a pen. In conditions of creativity that are increasingly complex, stringent editing can focus the multitasker's scuttling mind.

⌐

This book will not eliminate the need for an outside editor, but it will minimize it. When writers learn how to better edit themselves, editors will not be out of jobs; rather they will be working with texts at a more advanced stage, and their work will be less an act of excavation than one of refinement.

There is much pleasure, not just use, to editing yourself. Consider the high-pitched concentration and low-geared pace of a fine edit. The editing process is a dynamic one, even when enacted alone. If it isn't reaching into many directions at once, it isn't working. Editing involves a deep, long meditation within which the editor or self-editor listens to every last sound the prose before him makes, then separates the music from the noise. To edit, it is best to avoid putting yourself in a fully horizontal position, hungover, and imbibing coffee and chocolate as high-octane fuel that will speed you up, then burn you out. Writing and editing overlap, but by nature are not the same. Writing can tolerate—even gain from—mental vagary and vicissitude; editing, for the most part, cannot. Editing demands a yogi's physical stamina, flexibility, and steady mind.

There are those who believe that providing answers to a writer's questions or solutions to his errors is the definition of editing. Answers, however, halt the serpentine search that a writer often needs to make to solve a problem. New valuable ideas may appear during the search. This doesn't mean that an editor can't sometimes find the right word or phrase before a writer does. It happens. But the few words found can't compare to the verbal clusters a text needs that the writer alone can find. Answers are a very small part of the job. Guidance is the gist. A text deserves to be pondered and nudged, not simply bullied into place. No editor can, with crystal clarity, know the precise place her author's work ought to go. The editor's job is to sense the best direction by asking questions of the work; then to gently press or, if necessary, spur her writer there. Editing is a conversation, not a monologue. The wise self-editor will follow the example of the wise editor, and conduct an open-minded conversation with herself.

The Artful Edit will examine the very idea of editing, as well as offer techniques to rev up your editorial consciousness. In chapter one, we will learn to step back from our words to see them for what they are, not wish they would be. Chapters two and three will give us tools to track our text at both the micro- and macro-levels—with F. Scott Fitzgerald's *The Great Gatsby* as a model. In chapter four you will be invited into the studios of several writers and artists to watch the process of editing in action. This bird's-eye view is to freshen your notion of what editing can do, and as you watch the highly accomplished stumble before they walk, reassure you that you are not alone. In the final chapter we will comb history to see how editing evolved from ancient times. When we reach our era, we will watch editor Robin Robertson work with Adam Thorpe on his novel *Ulverton*. This contemporary edit acts as a counterpoint to the Perkins-Fitzgerald collaboration, and confirms that, despite the doomsayers, there are still, and I suspect always will be, a handful of editors who edit in earnest. The *Ulverton* edit also provides more wisdom about craft for self-editors.

Interspersed between the chapters are testimonies from an eclectic group of authors. Eliot Weinberger, Tracy Kidder, Ann Patchett, Scott Spencer, Harry Mathews, and Michael Ondaatje discuss how they edit themselves and what editing means to them. Their stylistic differences underscore the importance of editing: though each has a unique approach, all agree that careful self-editing is crucial.

These chapters and testimonies will prove that editing is as much an improvisation as a science; and the best self-editors and editors come to the act fearlessly attentive. Editing is more an attitude than a system. I will give you systematic methods that my students and I have found useful; but in the end, it is your open-mindedness, courage, and stamina that will make those methods function.

I
GAINING PERSPECTIVE

. . . if he knows well what he meant to do,
this knowledge always disturbs his perception
of what he has done.

Paul Valéry

A friend of mine, in the tenth and final year of writing a novel that would eventually win him the Rome Prize, was squirming as he made his way to the finish. While I wasn't worried about him—a writer generates anxiety as a lamp does heat—one of his anxieties startled and fascinated me. It did not have to do with an unwieldy chapter or concept. It resulted from the distance between the type of book he had set out to write and the type of book he had, in fact, written.

A passionate reader of irreverent forms of literature, Eli Gottlieb had set out to write a radical book. He loved the intricate narrative mechanisms of works by writers from James Joyce to John Hawkes, and he had wanted to write a book that would exude a kindred lack of convention. His book would perhaps be difficult to read, he knew, but it would be understood by a literary elite, and that would be enough.

What he wrote, however, was a novel that broke no conventions narratively, and adhered instead to classic linear storytelling.

His natural irreverence could be discerned, not in the formal aspect of the book, but in the voices of its characters.

The book's subject was the life of a family in suburban New Jersey, set off track by a developmentally disabled son. It was the story of two brothers, of a mother and her sons, of an alienated married couple, of a woman both loopy and shrewd trying to cope with life's traumas and disappointments. Though the subject itself had all the makings of melodrama (most subjects do), Gottlieb created an iridescent novel of character and wit: more Charles Dickens than Joyce, more Saul Bellow than Hawkes, but above all his own. Here is how *The Boy Who Went Away* begins:

I first noticed something strange happening to my mother six months earlier, in the motionless days of January. During a cold snap that turned everything the hue of smoke, her clothes suddenly began to grow bright, vivid, as if powered by a secret store of summer brilliance. Although it was frigid outside, her skirts shrank upward above the knees, while the heels of her shoes grew downward into spikes curved like the teeth of animals that made a rackety, military clatter on the floors of our house. I was sick with the flu for two weeks straight, and I noticed that with my father gone to work for the day, she would sometimes go upstairs and spend an hour carefully penciling freshness into her face—and then, to my amazement, leave on a long "run to the store." She seemed energized at strange times of the day, sparked into excited conversation by a random headline, a snatch of music on the Magnovox, or the blue of two jays she'd spotted tussling over seeds in the snow of our backyard. Bouncing as she walked, she would sometimes, for no obvious reason, come up to me and interrupt what I was doing to ask, "Front and center, Sweetness, how *are* you?"

One could argue that a simple structure was needed to show off the book's ranging wit and layered psychology. A simple room allows you to pay attention to its spectacular views, while one that is decorated lavishly may distract from them. An avant-garde form might have competed with, rather than supported, the novel's swivel-hipped humor and expansive heart. Might have. Might not have. We won't know what it would have been written differently, but we do know the book was successful written as it was. Measures of success are debatable—to finish a manuscript is a success. But Gottlieb's triumph is hard to dispute: If success means the author is satisfied with his work, Gottlieb was. If success means a book finds an appreciative audience, Gottlieb's did: his novel was, contrary to his original expectations, eminently readable, and loved by many more than a literary elite. *The Boy Who Went Away* was enjoyed by intellectuals (The American Academy of Rome) and nonintellectuals (my mother) alike.

Gottlieb had imagined his work sounding a certain way even before it was written, but as he wrote, he began to recognize and slowly accept that this story needed to be told on its own terms, not his. As novelist Jim Lewis puts it, "I stopped writing the book that I wanted to write, and wrote the one the book wanted to write." An editor, and a writer editing himself, must treat a work on its own terms. "The process is so simple," Max Perkins once told a crowded room of acolytes. "If you have a Mark Twain, don't try to make him into a Shakespeare or make a Shakespeare into a Mark Twain. Because in the end an editor can get only as much out of an author as the author has in him." The wise editor is agile and open, and never tries to turn a manuscript into something it is not meant to be. The wise writer, likewise, remains open to his work, and refrains from imposing an inorganic idea on it.

There are other books in Gottlieb that may coincide with his original conception of an avant-garde novel. If they do, it will not be simply because he wills them to, but because the material and moment call for it.

How did Gottlieb discover what his book wanted to be? How do you close the gap between an ideal you imagine for your text and the reality of the text that faces you? We all have writing or writers we admire and aspire to. It is not easy to abandon your ideal in order to accept what you perceive, at first, as your own meager self. It can take time to hear the power of your own voice, and until you do, you may keep hoping that you sound like George Eliot or Djuna Barnes, Stephen King or David Halberstam. Trying to sound like so-and-so is a fine exercise when you're building your chops, but once you start your work in earnest as a relatively mature writer, it is literary suicide. To write falsely is not to write at all.

An editor, a good one, reads to discover a new voice: a fresh sound in the ear, an as yet unmapped route to a particular emotion or thought. Surprise is the editor's drug of choice. A writer needs to relish the surprise of his own voice just as an editor does. Imagine: you read your draft, and as you move along, you have an uneasy sensation that it doesn't sound like anything else you've read. This may be because it is not working. But another possibility must be considered: your writing may sound strange to you because it is truly yours and no one else's; its strangeness is an indication of its honesty. In this case, you have hit your stride.

The awkward will become familiar as you commit to it, trust it, exploit it.

The veteran will suffer the same disorientation as the novice if he makes his text truly new. He will step beyond what he already knows and risk not recognizing his own voice. The difference between the veteran and novice, besides a mastery of craft, is confidence—or *the possibility of* confidence: the veteran might remember from previous experience that whatever is flawed can be fixed—more or less and with time; if it can't, it is not just flawed but inadequate, and deserves to perish, whether it weighs in light at thirty pages or heavy at three hundred. Under the veteran's feet is the floor of accomplishment, whereas the novice is walking on air.

But despite past achievements, the veteran can also become demoralized by his troublesome text. "Every writer I know suffers from the despondency of looking at his material," says D. S. Stone, a veteran screenwriter and journalist. Calmly or not, then, the author strains to see his work clearly, diagnose it, and begin revising. "The quality an artist must have," said Faulkner, "is objectivity in judging his work, plus the honesty and courage not to kid himself about it." Faulkner confessed, "I have written a lot and sent it off to print before I actually realized strangers might read it." It is fair to say that all writers—seasoned or not, steady or panicked—lose perspective.

So how can you tell if your writing is a gem or a trinket? There is, of course, no simple answer to this. You must achieve a transparent view of your material that derives from having emotional and psychological distance from it. With distance, you will be able to see what Gottlieb calls "the nervous system of the words in space"—how your words link together, what keeps them alive and how each affects another. The challenge is both physical and metaphysical. The metaphysical distance you get from your work will depend largely on your physical choices for it: to reread as you write or not; to leave your desk or not; to use a computer or not, and so on.

One distancing technique is to physically leave your desk without sneaking pages into your bag. This sounds easy, but any serious writer who has tried it knows that leaving your draft alone presents a profound challenge.

You could also rethink the virtue of rereading as you write. What would happen if you didn't allow yourself to go back to check your output, and only forged forward? You might not need a drastic rupture from your work at the end. You would have created an *ongoing distance* between you and your work; and your eyes, still fresh, would see pretty well as they read a finished draft.

"The greater the distance," writes W. G. Sebald in *The Rings of Saturn*, "the clearer the view: one sees the tiniest of details with the utmost clarity." Distance allows you to see your work. Different writers use different methods for attaining it. It is worth trying some of them—even, and perhaps especially, if they are initially uncomfortable. An alien method may rattle you awake to suddenly see an unfortunate aspect of your work that you have been avoiding.

THE PRINTOUT

A year after leaving a job as a full-time editor, a friend of mine found herself in Hanoi, where she began a novel. On her return to New York, she continued to write. The writing went well and not so well. The exuberance of exploring a new idea and voice propelled her. Some fine concepts were put into place and some fine phrasing seemed to write itself onto the page, as she was so loose and open; it was the beginning, and anything looked possible if she could stay the course.

Soon enough, however, she was producing fewer and fewer pages and feeling more and more muted. At one point, she realized she had been rereading and reworking the same two pages for six days. She had become obsessed with getting each page "right" before going on to the next. One day her husband suggested, ever so gently, that she stop tweaking each sentence to perfection as she went. "Yes, you're right," she said, and kept tweaking. A week later, he told her, gently but more firmly, "You really should stop rereading and redoing so much as you write." She nodded, and then once again ignored him. She now felt as if she were writing with a noose around her neck. Her husband knew what she was not ready to know: the professional editor in her had usurped the writer.

On the second trip to Hanoi, she brought her computer and a flimsy portable printer, which she could not get to print. Dismayed, she sat in her guesthouse room and wrote. On the fifth day she rejoiced. She could not print, so had no pages to reread and mark up. Forced by circumstance, she had written freely for days on end, rarely thinking about how it sounded. For the next three weeks, printerless, she concentrated on story and characters, not language, and felt liberated.

Many writers, like the one above, need to trust their language more from the start. They need to massage their story and characters (fictional or not) into being early on, and adjust their language later. To constantly print out, reread, and perfect your prose is usually a trap: after a month of writing, you often have perfectly laid out phrases that say very little, because you paid attention to their sound far more than their purpose.

We sometimes take the art of storytelling for granted. Stories—with their inevitable descriptions of family and friends—abound in daily life, at a dinner table or coffeehouse, for instance. But our daily narratives are more or less fragmented, only rudimentarily shaped. Although easy to tell them over a beer, it is hard labor to turn them into cohesive, dramatic writing. Natural bards exist, but they are not necessarily the best writers. Jack Kerouac was an exception. He constructed full stories in his head; he then wrote them quickly, faced only with the challenge of which words to use. He had already understood how the story would evolve. "You think out what actually happened," he once told *The Paris Review*, "you tell friends long stories about it, you mull it over in your mind, you connect it together at leisure, then when the time comes to pay the rent again you force yourself to sit at the typewriter, or at the writing notebook, and get it over with as fast as you can . . . and there's no harm in that because you've got the whole story lined up." This is hardly a universal model.

A great many authors determine the full shape of their stories *as* they write, not before. Story and characters make themselves clear as they unfold and move about. A narrative often follows a character's movement, instead of guiding it, so you cannot know your story perfectly at the start. Characters, like people, need freedom to err and rebound as they move forward. But if, when you write, you constantly check to make sure what you've done is good enough, you interrupt the élan and error your characters need to *become* good enough. You stymie your story before it can take flight.

Hanoi induced my friend's cure. She learned that if she didn't watch it, she would edit her writing into a lifeless specimen of overworked sentences, foreshortened story, and stunted characters. Editing is not writing, even if writing consists largely of editing. Indeed, premature and obsessive editing will destroy writing. For most, it is only with an unedited flow of imagination that there is anything worth revising in the end.

THE PEN

Judith Freeman is emphatic about sustaining a flow of imagination when she writes. By handwriting her novel *Red Water*, Freeman found detachment in the act of writing itself, not simply at the end of the draft. In the past, typing into a computer had made the writing process choppy. The flow of her imagination was continually blocked by frequent checking of sentences, paragraphs, words. By the end of a first draft, she would feel confused and drained by the continual rereads and minor adjustments she'd made along the way, and she would need a dramatic break from the text to see it clearly.

Freeman wanted to try another path to clarity: longhand. "When writing longhand," she explains,

the brain and the hand are connected. Once you begin to let an idea unfold, you keep unfolding it. Ink flows, ideas flow with it. When writing longhand, I am not tempted to constantly go back, scroll up, stop and reread. When you type, especially into a computer, you don't give your imagination the chance to really follow things through.

Clean and professional-looking, the typed page can induce the illusion that the sentences on it are finished and ready to be inspected. It is impossible to make that mistake with a hand-scrawled notebook. Moreover, the scroll mechanism of the word processor was a gilded invitation to Freeman's inner censor. Without the scroll, without clean type, Freeman relinquished her grip on her text. At the end of a draft, her words were essentially new to her. She hadn't read them to death by then, but just recorded them directly from her imagination. Or to use writer Albert Mobilio's phrase, it was "as if [her] hands were the actual agents of composition." After she had finished the handwritten draft, Freeman transferred it from her notebooks into her computer, then used the ease of a computer processor to edit further drafts.

Not everyone will be willing or able to write in longhand. Using a pen will seem too anachronistic, quaint, and above all, inefficient. But don't form rash conclusions before you give it a try. Freeman proved that longhand can be as or more efficient than a word processor. Her editor made far fewer suggestions on *Red Water*, for instance, than on her previous computer-written manuscripts. For Freeman, there were three advantages to longhand: (1) Slowing down in the writing stage made her first draft more thought-out. (2) Because she didn't constantly reread as she wrote, her first reread was fresh; so she saw more clearly and more quickly what needed adjustment. (3) The kinetic link from a writer's mind to ink to page seemed to make Freeman's first draft truer to what she wanted, so there were fewer changes than usual. Freeman credits the pen with her ability to see her manuscript clearly and edit it well herself before handing it to an editor.

Whereas Freeman gave up the computer to write more fluidly, D. S. Stone, who uses one, says, "I never reread what I'm working on while I'm working on it. The less I look at [my writing], when it is time to edit it, the fresher I am." He follows Freeman's dictum, but goes at it differently. Stone has taught himself, after years of application, to type with a flow reminiscent of Freeman's longhand. The potentially alienating machine that divides hand from word does not disturb him. "You do the thing and get it done," he says, the ultimate pragmatist.

Echoing Stone, Jonathan Franzen says,

> I've learned to avoid rewriting on the computer screen until I have a complete draft of a section or chapter. By then, a good deal of time has passed, and I can see the pages more clearly. Generally, if I find myself trying to achieve perspective prematurely . . . it's a sign that the section isn't working and that I don't want to admit this to myself.

To avoid rereading as you type, try writing with a pen. If you resist writing with a pen, try harder to resist the scroll mechanism on your computer.

THE CLOCK

Once Stone has finished his draft, he will not allow more than a day to pass before rereading it. Stepping back for more than a day allows him to ruminate on other projects and thereby lose interest in the one at hand. Momentum is more important to Stone than the extra perspective he might gain from a long break. He believes that every piece of writing has an internal clock: "there is a certain amount of time allotted to a piece before you lose sight of your instincts, of what you're trying to say; and [when you work on something for too long] another part of you comes out that's meaner, more unpleasant." An attuned, compassionate self-editor exists within Stone, that, Cinderella-like, disappears after the hour is too late.

Writers disagree on how to banish the inner censor, but all

would agree that banish it they must. Every writer has to discover his best protection from a rapacious internal judge.

THE BIG BREAK

Albert Mobilio, writer (*Me with Animal Towering*) and fiction editor of *Bookforum*, has learned to accommodate his obsession with polishing: "I tend to revise a lot while writing. I used to throw away a dozen sheets with first sentences; now I just type over and micro-revise constantly."

To make substantive changes in his rich, pellucid prose, he waits days or weeks, but notes that deadline work often precludes the luxury of a breather. Gottlieb, like Mobilio, writes and edits with a jeweler's eye for minuscule linguistic details, and at the same time develops the larger design. The two writers agree that the longer the break at the end of a draft, the better. They take weeks off, when possible, to more clearly see the big picture.

Make a choice. Choose to write in longhand, on a manual typewriter, or on a computer; do not submit to one, as if it were an inevitability. If obsessive rereading is impeding your progress, stop printing hard copy for a time. If, conversely, you like to edit the details along the way, securing each bezel before you set another stone, take a sizable break at the end of your draft before you reread and diagnose what more it needs. In short, if you achieve distance along the way, you'll need less at the end; if you do not achieve distance along the way, you'll need more at the end.

On principle, check your impulse to reread and revise at every turn. You will benefit doublefold: your imagination will have room to stretch out, and your brain will be fresher when called on to edit. But for some, it will be unnatural to wait. No method is incorrect. If you keep working, every method will lead you to a finished manuscript. Try, however, to find the one that works for, more than against, you.

THE SPOKEN WORD

Bradford Morrow speaks of reading one's work aloud with the fervor of the religiously converted. "There are things that the ear sees that the eye can't hear," he says. Writer (*Ariel's Crossing*) and editor of *Conjunctions* magazine, Morrow did not always recite his own words to himself. But after having written a few novels, he tried it and found that reading aloud was a prime tool for gaining perspective.

Reading one's work aloud is hardly a new idea. From Homer to the Norse epics, stories were told, not read; and through the telling they were edited. Before the fifteenth century, authorship and therefore editing were necessarily communal. Without a printing press, bards and the public itself were the writer's distribution service. A story was a direct gift to the community, and as it was shared aloud, retold and retold, the story transformed into something other than the author's original.

We cannot know what changes were made orally, since they were not recorded. We can, however, bear witness to some shocking changes made when pioneer publishers—still influenced by a recent culture of bards—made freewheeling edits. In the eighteenth century, Samuel Johnson, acting as textual critic, discovered that the line in Shakespeare's *Hamlet* "In private to inter him" had originally been "In hugger mugger to inter him." The latter had been considered inelegant and got the editor's ax. Johnson replaced the original passage, defending his move: "That the words now replaced are better, I do not undertake to prove: it is sufficient that they are Shakespeare's." Johnson argues for the integrity of a single author's work: "If phraseology is to be changed as words grow uncouth by disuse, or gross by vulgarity, the history of every language will be lost; we shall no longer have the works of any author; and, as these alterations will be often unskillfully made, we shall in time have very little of his meaning." Johnson's was a modern view, in keeping with a future he could overhear before it spoke. Today we place a tremendous value on the original text written by the author alone.

Now that stories are the reflection of a single author, not an oral community, editing occurs in the writer's or editor's office, not, hip-hop aside, on the street corner. If the very zeitgeist of writing has changed, one aspect of it hasn't. Reading aloud was an editing tool then, and still is. "It's almost impossible," V. S. Naipaul told an interviewer, "to read one's work. One can never read it as a stranger." To alleviate the problem, he added, "I've always read my day's work aloud." Naipaul would read aloud to himself. Some find it more useful to read aloud to a friend—another person's presence can make certain writers climb farther outside themselves to see their work from a distance, from where it always appears clearer.

As far back as the first century A.D., writers understood and wrote about the editorial value of reading work aloud. Public readings, fashionable in that time, "were meant to bring the text not only to the public but back to the author as well," writes Alberto Manguel in his superb book *A History of Reading*. Pliny the Younger "sometimes tried out a first draft of a speech on a group of friends and then altered it according to their reaction," writes Manguel. In ancient Rome, reading aloud involved a precise etiquette in which listeners were, he notes, "expected to provide critical response, based on which the author would improve the text." Readings could be for a small group of friends or for a large anonymous public. Or as with Molière in the seventeenth century, who regularly read his plays aloud to one person, his housemaid. Nineteenth-century novelist Samuel Butler eluci- dated in his *Notebooks*:

> If Molière ever did read to her, it was because the mere act of reading aloud put his work before him in a new light and, by constraining his attention to every line, made him judge it more rigorously. I always intend to read, and gen- erally do read, what I write aloud to someone; anyone almost will do, but he should not be so clever that I am afraid of him. I feel weak places at once when I read aloud where I thought, as long as I read to myself only, that the passage was all right.

Public readings are still useful these days for both publicity and editing—though most contemporary writers will not display the malleability of their writing. They read it as if it is set in stone, and later, in private, jot down the weak points that their reading out revealed to them. But one need not risk public humiliation to gain the editorial benefits of reading aloud. For as Butler explains, it is "the mere act" of reading aloud that aids; it is not the audience's critique, but the author's revitalized attention to his words through uttering them and hearing them uttered that brings clarity.

Mobilio learned the hard way: "I've had the experience of giv- ing readings and wincing at sentences that seemed freshly askew to me as they rolled off my tongue. This led to making *in medias res* edits that only broke my flow and furthered my dismay." He therefore began a reading series, as it were, in the privacy of his own home, with no one but himself in the audience. He is able to become on his own a pseudostranger, like the "stranger" Naipaul wishes to become for himself. "The best way to change places with your imagined reader," says Mobilio, "is to read out loud and really hear your own too familiar words; enunciation makes their jostle or flow, sense or silliness palpable as touch."

Intoned, your text becomes dynamic, whereas inside your head it was still; the clunky or obtuse parts fall out like so many bolts that weren't well fastened, and couldn't be detected until you started to speak.

When you first recite your words to yourself (or anyone else), the peculiar sound of your own voice and the familiar sound of your words might combine to disorient you. Feeling awkward may dull your execution, and make it impossible to know if it is your text or your reading that is flawed. So while you do not need to ape your story in dramatic relief, it helps to read with conviction.

You might try two variations of reading aloud that I learned from my students. One, record yourself and play it back. Two, get a neutral friend or family member to read your text to you. (Family members are by definition not neutral, but you may know the rare one who can surmount, or at least silence, his prejudices for thirty minutes. One student prefers that a philistine read her work to her—she does not want to be seduced by the dramatic inflections a literary reader might impart.) To hear your words in a strange voice will instantly divest you of them. They will seem to belong to the reader, not you, and this will help you hear them better.

THE FONT

W. H. Auden used to say, rather pungently, that he could only truly "see" a poem once it's typed because "a man likes his own handwriting the way he likes the smell of his own farts." Type creates a famously useful distance between the writer and his words. But most contemporary writers are inured to type, having seen their manuscript take shape in it from the start. Non-handwriters need a new device to make their work look new.

Jim Lewis discovered that going from Times Roman to Helvetica kicked the complacency out of his eye. What the eye sees newly, so does the brain. At the end of a draft, Lewis prints out his manuscript in an alternate type font. Try it on one paragraph. The shift in perspective can be dramatic.

THE ENVIRONMENT

Writer Tom McDonough, author of *Light Years*, suggests changing your surroundings to edit. Read your work someplace other than where you wrote it. A change of venue freshens the spirit; why wouldn't it freshen the mind's critical eye too? You might arrange for a short stay at a friend's house down the road or in another city. You might bring your draft to another country. If you wrote at your office desk, the kitchen table might be a better place for editing.

McDonough has edited while traveling with great success. "When your environment is different, and your activity is different," he says, "you bring this thing with you that's looked the same for so long, and it looks different, too." You could take this idea one step further and change your daily habits as well as geography. Edit at night, for instance, instead of in the day. If you always wait for a clear few weeks to edit in, try editing instead alongside another job. McDonough decided to edit his novel *Virgin with Child*, for example, at night after working all day as a cinematographer, instead of the usual at home between jobs. Making money and working hard hours put him, he says, in a "pragmatic mind-set"; he had no time or inclination to indulge himself or his prose.

THE RELEASE

Once you let it out of your protective grasp, your manuscript loses the seductive patina that, because it has been fondled so much, settled on it. Suddenly it appears garish without the soft gleam lent by your continual touch, or by *the possibility of* your touch, which is just as powerful as the touch itself; just knowing you can get at the thing again reassures you and makes your work look better to you. When we edit, we see our manuscript through a split lens: through one half, we view what is really there; through the other, what could be. The bifocal mind is a wishful mind and skews the work's potential for greatness into greatness itself.

When you get the manuscript out of the house, you temporarily put a lid on potential. The process stops. The manuscript has become, it is no longer becoming. A subtle but serious psychological shift occurs in the author: he sees his work through a single lens now, the one that shows him what is really there.

Sending out your manuscript to an agent or editor can be the most terrifying and cruelest of methods for gaining perspective. But it will, without fail, get you to see your words through a stranger's eyes. Because after you send it you will not be able to keep from rereading it, and from trying to put yourself in your reader's mind. From this leap of imagination, you will learn a lot about your text.

One writer I know had his agent send out a "finished" section of his novel, in an attempt to sell it. The day after it went out to publishers, he reread it. In a cold sweat, he telephoned the agent and, after some debate, demanded that she retract the submission, which she did. He had seen it, all of a sudden, from the perspective of a stranger—the editors who were about to read it—and he knew, as he hadn't been able to know until then, that it was all wrong. It isn't always another person's critique that helps you see your manuscript clearly (your reader may be dead wrong). It is the very fact of sending the work out that forces you to look at it differently.

I am not encouraging you to go to the post office tomorrow to send off unfinished work. But if you feel very close to having finished, and you cannot go any further, then you may want to risk it. But it really is a risk. If an agent or editor doesn't like it, it will be hard to get a second read from him later.

The best alternative is to send it to a friend. You will benefit in a similar but not as stark manner. You will have to sift through your intimate knowledge of your reader to find the part of him that is somehow still a stranger—it is the stranger in your friend who counts, and with whom you will identify when you reread the work. Eventually, when you hear from your friendly reader, keep in mind his personal agenda and taste; filter his comments through your knowledge of his prejudices (including his predisposition to like whatever you do). But in the end, it isn't his response that really matters here. The mere fact that he is in possession of your text could help you achieve a fresh perspective on it.

THE INNER CENSORATE

Another trick for seeing the text through someone else's eyes—without the risk of letting it out of the house—is what Auden called the Inner Censorate. Think of specific people you are writing to; pretend you are reading your text through their eyes. According to Auden, this watchdog organization "should include, for instance, a sensitive only child, a practical housewife, a logician, a monk, an irreverent buffoon and even, perhaps, hated by all the others and returning their dislike, a brutal, foul-mouthed drill sergeant who considers all poetry rubbish."

Writer Luc Sante (*Low Life*) has used the technique: "I've always relied on an internal Censorate composed of people I know and people I've met who made a certain kind of impression on me. I read my work through the eyes of people of very different temperament and taste, always including a genuine poet, a very intelligent person with no formal education and no patience with literary posturing, and someone who knows more about the subject than I do."

The Censorate is the monitor that tells you when you've gone too pedantic, flat-footed, or vague. However, you should not create an Inner Censorate unless you are capable of quieting the din of its often conflicting voices and returning to your individual sense of what works. Beware of the temptation to pander. If your Censorate overtakes you, stop listening to it altogether.

Wait until the end of a draft before you turn to your Inner Censorate. This editing technique should never interfere with writing itself.

THE CONVERSATION

A gallerist called me with a job. I was to edit an essay by art critic Neville Wakefield, whom I had edited before. A week later we sat in his office and, via a rich conversation that often turned into debate, addressed my questions about his text. We each held a copy of the edited manuscript. I queried and commented. Wakefield answered and asked his own questions. Once we were both satisfied with an alternate phrasing, he typed it into his computer.

This kind of collaborative revision will not work for some

writers who need to reflect at length and privately on their final version. But for many, conversation can be a marvelous tool for revision. It is especially helpful for magazine writers who face tight deadlines and have no time to step away from their draft. The mutually active editorial conversation demands high concentration from both parties, and a relinquishment of ego. A writer whose words are priceless possessions to be protected from what he perceives as an editor's insensitive hand should not try it. A writer like Wakefield, who wants to communicate his ideas more than cling to his words for the sake of it, will benefit. When there is a gap between what he means to say and what he has said, for example, Wakefield permits a respectful editor to help him modulate the text to close that gap.

Here is how it worked with Wakefield and me:

To familiarize you with his writing, it helps to think about art criticism at large, where empty rhetoric abounds. A few critics, though, write complex prose that *says* something. Wakefield is one. His rhythmic improvisations and verbal flourishes continually return to a rigorous central argument, where understanding is visceral, not simply intellectual.

The main point of his essay, when I received it, was hard to understand. He was writing about Japanese photographer Daido Moriyama's New York pictures from 1971, which were radical for the time. Grainy and indistinct, they were more like sensations than photographs. Wakefield had written a piece to evoke, not describe or explain, these pictures. The piece began as if it were the continuance of something that had begun before, and ended as if it kept going after the reader left. The fragmented, fugitive feel of the prose matched the fragmented, fugitive feel of the images. Nonetheless, the piece kept sliding away from me as I read it; a clarity of purpose was missing; and besides, I couldn't readily tell who was doing what, which left me, in the most pedestrian sense, confused.

His first lines originally read:

> Dark with something more than night, New York 1971 is a city of shadows, caught in the radar sweep of a vision that obliterates as it reveals. Taken without heed to the accepted protocols, the chance condensations of light mix evidence with abstraction. Like that radar sweep that obliterates as it reveals they go against the grain of traditon. They record less the monuments that loom all around, than the transient ephemeral social architecture that fills the intermittent spaces—

How far could Wakefield go with imprecise references before his reader would feel lost and lose interest? Moriyama's photographs were imprecise, but an essay functions differently from a photograph. Imprecision, in literary matters, dulls or befuddles the reader. My task was to help Wakefield make his piece more accessible, without relinquishing its affective mimicry of Moriyama's shards and shadows. To be of help meant to respect the poetry of the essay, so that the reader's understanding would be sensual as well as intellectual—or as poet Ann Lauterbach puts it, understanding would come "thru the agency of a musical syntax, where what can be apprehended as sense and what can be apprehended beyond sense are inseparable."

I asked the writer if he would shorten the first sentence to make it more inviting; it held too many different and elusive ideas for the reader to grasp right off. I also suggested building up to its swirling rhythm. I asked whose "vision" it was in the first sentence. Wakefield realized this was unclear, but he didn't want to mention Moriyama's name at all in the piece so he cut the vision part out. I suggested that "Taken" in the second sentence was ambiguous. He replaced it with "Shot," which referred more clearly to making photographs. "The chance condensations of light" became "these chance condensations of light": now they would refer to a particular set of pictures. "Radar sweep" in sentence three repeats without good reason "radar sweep" in sentence one. Wakefield chose to keep the later one. I asked him to pinpoint the meaning of the radar sweep in this essay; it seemed to have loose threads that were catching on other ideas and tangling them all up. So he separated one idea from another, and in the process let one drop. I thought "transient ephemeral social architecture that fills the intermittent spaces" was adjective heavy—especially with these academic-sounding adjectives. He tossed out "transient" and "ephemeral" and put "intermittent" in their place. And so on.

Here is our edited version:

> Dark with something more than night, New York 1971 is a city of shadows. Shot without heed to the accepted protocols, these chance condensations of light mix evidence with abstraction. Like the radar sweep, they obliterate as they reveal. They record less the monuments that loom all around, than the intermittent social architecture that fills the spaces in between—

The photographer's images of New York, and the writer's evocation of them, still meld; we simply follow Wakefield's meaning more clearly now.

The two-person editorial conversation, even if you don't use it, is a good model for an internal editorial dialogue. The push and pull of a dual exchange can be replicated inside one writer's mind. Mark up your text like an editor would, and go through each query more or less systematically, hashing out with yourself each ambiguity or conundrum.

THE HANG-UP OR LAY-OUT

Twenty-five years ago, I visited an artist's colony set in the woods of southern France. From that visit, I kept the memory of a string that stretched across the length of one poet's studio. He had hung his poems up, like a recent load of laundry, and read them standing or pacing around. The sight of paper sheets waving in the breeze made an impression on me, and I knew I'd have to try it. A few years later, I strung a line through my New York apartment and hung up my pages. I have had a cord strung across my workspace ever since.

There are many benefits to the line method. There is the increased alertness you feel when you read on your feet, as well as the disorientation—we're not used to reading upright, and the novelty of it helps make our material feel new.

Also, to read pages horizontally is quite different from reading them in a stack, where you see only one page at a time. You can see proportions better when you read across, page to page to page, glancing back and forth, and stepping back to take in a view of the whole typographic design of a chapter. You will more easily see whether you've used too many tiny or lengthy paragraphs in one area. If you have a specific concern, use a highlighter or the bold key on your computer to make it stand out, then hang the pages up and observe where the color or bold type is either dense or absent—this may tell you if there is too little of one person, for instance, too much of one verb, too little dialogue, or too much of a leitmotiv.

On hearing of the laundry-line method, Laura Kipnis, author of *Against Love*, said, "O no, I could never do that. I have to lay it all out on the floor." She walks or crawls around on top of her pages, reading and moving them as pieces of a puzzle.

Jim Lewis tapes his pages to the wall. He will print his manuscript out in a tiny, unreadable font size, so he can hang the entire book up. He will look at it like a painting or a map, searching for topographical imbalances.

Whichever way you choose—cord and clips, wall and tape, or floor—it can be valuable when you edit to look at your manuscript's topography.

⌒

Perspective meant one thing for Eli Gottlieb, another for Neville Wakefield. Gottlieb needed to gain perspective on the true nature of his novel, whereas Wakefield knew what kind of essay he wanted to write, but needed perspective on the words and syntax he had used to write it. Gottlieb questioned the whole, that is, and Wakefield the minutiae. For the novelist, some of the above-listed methods helped, including the "big break." The critic, cornered by a deadline, could not take a big break. "Conversation" served Wakefield instead. Perhaps his essay demanded less distance than Gottlieb's fiction. Fiction's lack of guidelines in the external world can make its achievement exceedingly hard to assess. In any genre, though, perspective refers to the whole body of a text and its microscopic details. Depending on the kind of writer you are, and the situation you are up against, use the appropriate method to find perspective on your writing.

We will always need outside readers to see what we, on our own, cannot. But the ideal reader is not always around when you need him, and so depending on him is risky. Without an editor to give you a professional opinion, you must depend on yourself. Patience is key: do not be in a big hurry to finish. Give yourself time to be wrong and, then, eventually come round to understanding what's right. In her journals about making art, painter Agnes Martin writes: "defeat is the beginning, not the end of all positive action." With time, and editorial technique, we will discover, *on our own*, the difference between the piece we intend and the one we must write; between what we think we are supposed to do, usually to satisfy some false idea of what others want from us—in Gottlieb's case, to be avant-garde—and what we need to do. Perspective may seem impossible to achieve, but achieving it is essential.

METHODS FOR GAINING PERSPECTIVE

1. **The Printout:** Do not print out before you have a finished section or chapter. You may even wait until you've finished the book.

2. **The Pen:** If you normally type, try writing longhand instead. If you use a computer, do not scroll back as you write.

3. **The Clock:** Edit before too much time passes, especially if you risk losing interest in a project after you've moved on to another.

4. **The Big Break:** Take the longest break possible before you edit.

5. **The Spoken Word:** Read aloud to yourself or a select audience.

6. **The Font:** Change fonts when you print out.

7. **The Environment:** Edit someplace other than where you wrote.

8. **The Release:** Give the manuscript to a reader you take seriously.

9. **The Inner Censorate:** Create an Inner Censorate of imagined or real people who you want to satisfy.

10. **The Conversation:** Let yourself be edited on the spot through conversation and improvisation.

11. **The Hang-up or Lay-out:** Hang your manuscript on a laundry line, tape it to the wall, or lay it on the floor: Peruse for proportions, rhythm, leitmotivs, continuity, etc. Consider the topography of your book.

PRACTICE: PERSPECTIVE WITH AN OPEN MIND

This exercise encourages an awareness of your blind spots as a reader. It also hones precision of thought and expression, which an editor sorely needs.

1. Name one or two of your favorite books and explain why you love them.

Example: One of my favorite books is Melville's *Moby-Dick* because it is big and complex. I love big books you can sink into for a long time. I like to travel to other periods and places when I read, and learn about worlds I am unfamiliar with, such as the sea and whaling in the nineteenth century. For me, the magic of reading is in being transported outside myself, my immediate surroundings, and what I already know. I also love *Moby-Dick* for its linguistic muscle, metaphors, and spiritual dimension.

2. Reflect: Do you read with standards of quality or an agenda of taste?

As readers, we too easily dismiss writing that does not adhere to our habitual taste. We form an agenda based on what we most naturally love or gravitate to. If, in other words, the above fan of *Moby-Dick* started in on a short novel about a suburban family set in modern times that focused on a single character and had spare, pithy descriptions—say, John O'Hara's *Appointment in Samarra* or Alice McDermott's *That Night*—he might put it down after five pages, however well written, because it wasn't long, overtly complex, historical, or brimming with detail. He might, in other words, reject a radiant mesa in his search for majestic mountains.

Do not impose your taste on the text set before you, be it your own or another's. Ask not, is this my kind of writing? Ask, is this working? Is this working on its own terms?

While an editor at Random House, I learned about my own prejudices when I read a manuscript called *The Angel Carver* by Rosanne Daryl Thomas. I began the novel at my office and, twenty pages in, thought, "Nah, this isn't my thing. Too commercial, too easy." At the time, my editorial agenda was "high literature" which, in my youth, meant, as much as anything else, difficult to read. At home, I opened the book again (out of mere curiosity I told myself) and when I finished it at 3:00 A.M. I knew I would publish it. The chiseled prose and sure pacing gripped me. The novel was an adult fable that could be turned inside out into a feminist allegory. More commercial than other books I loved, it was also well wrought, engaging, and inventive. Who was I to snub *that*? "Preoccupation with the quality of one's taste," as writer Steve Erickson says, "is the way of small and cautious spirits." Relinquish your dogmatic agenda, be it highfalutin or lowriding. Listen to what moves you, and if it isn't what you expect, rejoice in the surprise.

As Tight as a Legal Brief
Eliot Weinberger

I always thought Flaubert was totally normal when he spent all morning putting in a comma, and then all afternoon erasing it. That seems totally normal to me.

I don't allow myself to be edited. I write very slowly and I spend a lot of time worrying about every comma. It's a thin line, at this point, between copy editing and line editing. I feel that I have idiosyncratic ways of using punctuation and things like that, but it's not because I'm ignorant; it's because I know the rules, but I want to do it a different way.

I have my editor at New Directions, Peter Glassgold, whom I've worked with for thirty years and who is wonderful in that he knows all my idiosyncrasies. He doesn't try to change anything, but he's very good for pointing out genuine mistakes. I like it when editors point out genuine mistakes and obviously you want an editor who is enthusiastic about what you write. Enthusiasm is important. Because what do you do when you're a writer? You sit around in a room all day, so it's nice to have somebody say something nice to you.

I remember once when I translated [Jorge Luis] Borges's essays, a prestigious literary magazine was going to publish one of them, which was three pages long. They wanted to cut a paragraph out of it. They said that they thought the reader's attention flagged in that paragraph. I said, ". . . if the reader's bored for one paragraph, by the time they get to the next paragraph, they'll wake up again." It's that ridiculous idea that you have to be thrilled every second.

⌒

It's interesting that the word editor—in the American sense—does not exist in other languages. For example, the policy in Latin America with magazines is that you pretty much sink or swim according to what you wrote. They correct spelling mistakes and obvious things like that, but they pretty much publish it the way you wrote it. The result is that any given magazine has a much greater diversity of voices than American magazines have. There's a greater diversity of quality, too, but there's a greater diversity of voices, unlike American magazines that all end up sounding as though they were written by the same person because the editor keeps rewriting the piece. Because they have a house style. Everything gets poured into the mold. It doesn't matter what the subject is. Everything has to be in that beautifully polished prose. The editors sort of throw it into the Cuisinart and it all comes out sounding the same.

⌒

When you're young is when you're supposed to be writing your most outlandish things, the things that are going to really embarrass you later on, and where you really try out things and experiment. The problem with the creative writing class is that you're being judged by your peers, so there's inevitable self-censorship involved. In subtle ways, people start editing themselves according to what is essentially a house style of whatever that creative writing class is. Possibly there are teachers who can respect all kinds of writing, but then the other students tend to be conservative. So it's very hard.

⌒

I always think that translation is one of the best ways to learn how to write, because you get involved in the nuts and bolts of how a line of poetry is written, or how a sentence of prose is written without the embarrassment, without the psychological dimensions, without the "Here I am expressing myself. Is it good enough? Is it bad?" You can learn so much technique from translation.

Editing is about becoming a reader. And that's the thing with translation. There are many people who prefer themselves in translation, like Gabriel García Márquez and Octavio Paz, who said, "I have doubts about myself in Spanish, but I love myself in English." The reason why is because they get to read themselves as readers in a way that you don't when you're looking at your own stuff. It's interesting to read yourself in translation, because the defects in the original become readily apparent. As soon as it's translated into a different language, you immediately see what's wrong. You see what really comes through and what doesn't come through.

I'm from the school of Charles Reznikoff, who said that every line of his poetry should be as solid as a line in a legal brief. Whenever I write a sentence, I try to think if the opposite of what I just said is true, and I try to think of all the objections that could be made to that statement. This idea of making it as tight as a legal brief is very helpful.

Basically, you have an infinite variety of ways in which people write, all of which are valid, and in the end, none of which matter because what matters is the final product. Some people write at night, some people write in the morning. In terms of editing, you have some people who write a lot, and then they have to cut out a lot. It's that Thomas Wolfe thing where you begin with a lot of writing and then you have to cut it down.

I work in the absolute opposite way, which is that I write very little and then keep adding to it and adding to it, and I almost never cut out anything. Sometimes if things are veering off in the wrong direction, I'll cut out a phrase. I move things around, but I basically don't cut much, so the thing grows organically very slowly. It's growing in my head, it's growing on the paper. Everything I write goes through dozens and dozens and dozens of drafts. I'm adding, and I'm changing words, but mainly I'm adding.

The thing that really changed my life was word processing. I was a two-finger typist. It would take me forever to type things, so I didn't used to edit myself very much because I didn't want to have to retype it. Now, with word processing, of course that changes everything, so I end up doing at least a draft a day. It's better—I work a lot harder because I don't have to spend all my time typing.

I write on the screen and I correct on the screen, but I also print out at least every day. I write and write on the screen, then at a certain point I have to see it on paper and then on paper I always see things that I didn't see on the screen. Then it goes through more corrections. Then, I let it sit around for a while. Even when I think it's good, I let it sit around for a while.

⸺

About fifteen years ago, when I was putting together a book of essays, I sent the manuscript to two people I really respect, who are brilliant and wonderful writers, to get their opinions on it. What *each one said was the complete opposite of what the other said. One said, "This essay is the best essay in the book. It's fabulous." The other guy said, "This is the worst essay in the book. You really should cut it out." Their responses cancelled each other out, so I ignored both of them and went back to what I was doing in the first place.*

II

THE BIG PICTURE: MACRO-EDITING

What a bitch of a thing prose is!
Flaubert

A woman has relinquished herself to a marriage of material ease. Her husband, of Herculean build and boorish mind, does not love her as much as the idea of her. Betrayal like a breeze wafts through their house, which overlooks a great lawn and, beyond it, an ocean.

A stranger comes to town. His wealth is obvious, its origins mysterious; most assume he is corrupt, but no one stays away from him because of it. He gives lavish parties to lure the unhappily married woman, whom he secretly loves . . .

And so on.

The summary above does not hint at the triumph of F. Scott Fitzgerald's novel *The Great Gatsby*. We all know the book—we were forced to read it for high school English. Like most books thrust upon students as another cut in the key that will release them from the prison of formal education, it has an ambiguous luster. We remember we liked it, but we're not sure if our admiration was sincere or derived from a desire to please the teacher and get out.

An informal survey of my acquaintances suggests that very few adults have read *Gatsby* lately. When I reread it in the spring of 2002, at the age of forty-three, I hadn't looked at it in nearly thirty years. My earliest reading of *Gatsby* had been supplanted by images of Robert Redford and Mia Farrow, film having usurped literature, as Fitzgerald himself predicted it would.

I was reminded of this eminent but taken-for-granted novel when I read the biography of Max Perkins by A. Scott Berg. Perkins and Fitzgerald enjoyed one of history's most rewarding editor-writer collaborations. Berg gives a fine account of how Perkins and Fitzgerald, together, refined *The Great Gatsby*. Perkins's influence was limited, Berg notes, because "[Fitzgerald] is generally regarded as having been his own best editor, as having had the patience and objectivity to read his words over and over again, eliminating flaws and perfecting his prose." Fitzgerald relied on Perkins, then, not for a line-to-line edit, as did Thomas Wolfe, but for counsel on structure and character—in other words, for a macro-edit.

Though limited, Perkins's help was far from incidental. "I had rewritten *Gatsby* three times," Fitzgerald freely admitted, "before Max said something to me. Then I sat down and wrote something I was proud of." The macro-edit, more conceptual in nature than a detailed edit, was crucial to him.

Before we look at Perkins's critique and Fitzgerald's revision, I should say why I chose to discuss *Gatsby* and not another novel. In truth, the book chose me. When I read it on a whim to see how it matched Berg's account of its making, I was floored. Every sentence and event felt necessary. Fitzgerald managed to fuse ultramodern prose—taut, symbolic, elliptical—with splendid lyricism: ornate, fluid descriptions of parties, for example, that rival Tolstoy's descriptions of war. *Gatsby* is a case study of Flaubertian froideur—

the cold that burns. Finally, and heroically, Fitzgerald maintained compassion for a humanity he portrayed in the most sinister terms.

My interest was editing, though, not just writing, and the author's painstaking edit of *Gatsby* distinguished it. It is, quite simply, a tour de force of revision. So much so that critics, who rarely mention the edit of a book, pointed to the quality of Fitzgerald's rewriting, not just writing, in reviews. For H. L. Mencken, the novel had "a careful and brilliant finish. . . . There is evidence in every line of hard and intelligent effort. . . . The author wrote, tore up, rewrote, tore up again. There are pages so artfully contrived that one can no more imagine improvising them than one can imagine improvising a fugue." Gilbert Seldes agreed: "*The Great Gatsby* is a brilliant work, and it is also a sound one; it is carefully written, and vivid; it has structure, and it has life. To all the talents, discipline has been added." Careful, sound, carefully written; hard effort; wrote and rewrote, artfully contrived not improvised; structure, discipline: all these terms refer, however obliquely, not to the initial act of inspiration, but to willful editing.

Gatsby's splendors are obviously the result of Fitzgerald's talent, but for our investigation into self-editing, let's put the question of talent aside. "*The Great Gatsby* achieved greatness through extensive proof revisions," Fitzgerald scholar Matthew Bruccoli reminds. There is a saying: Genius is perseverance. While genius does not consist entirely of editing, without editing it's pretty useless.

⌒

There are two types of editing: the ongoing edit and the draft edit. Most of us edit as we write and write as we edit, and it's impossible to slice cleanly between the two. You're writing, you change a word in a sentence, write three sentences more, then back up a clause to change that semicolon to a dash; or you edit a sentence and a new idea suddenly spins out from a word change, so you write a new paragraph where until that moment nothing else was needed. That is the ongoing edit. (See chapter one for help with the obsessive spiral that often accompanies it.)

For the draft edit, you stop writing, gather a number of pages together, read them, make notes on what works and doesn't, then rewrite. It is only in the draft edit that you gain a sense of the whole and view your work as a detached professional. It is the draft edit that makes us uneasy, and that arguably matters most.

There are three types of self-editors: (1) *Arrogant and blind*: You believe you are a master and that masters only commit very few and very minor errors. Your worst missteps remain hidden behind your conceited idea of yourself and your mistaken idea of what constitutes a master. (2) *Panicked and too timid or too aggressive*: You overestimate the problems of your text and lose heart before you begin. You edit too timidly (afraid to face what's wrong) or too aggressively (convinced that everything is wrong). (3) *Pragmatic and cool*: You are possessed by the need to make your writing function. You consider yourself neither genius nor idiot. You edit like the French recommend exacting revenge: coldly.

In this chapter and the next, we will study the two views—macro and micro—that pragmatic self-editors must apply to any manuscript. Within these two views, narrative elements function like settings on a camera lens. As you examine your work, turn the lens, and check how your writing looks at each setting.

Ideally, we would first look through the macro-, then the micro-lens: view the big picture, then focus on details. But reading and writing are not systematic. In reality, a person switches from lens to lens as she reads, her eye catching a jumble of images at once. You may, when you edit, try to train the eye to see more or less in sequence. But never expect, nor wish to achieve, a rigid artificial system. Reading must remain as free as the imagination itself. If you control your reading too much, you cease to be involved in it. Then what's the point?

Another reason not to read too methodically is that a strict method will force a text into categories too cleanly divided. Character here, leitmotiv there. Theme here, continuity of style there. But narrative parts work in tandem. They dovetail, and as with people in love, it can be impossible to see where one ends and the other begins. Try too hard to separate the parts and you destroy the whole. Allow, rather, the natural integration of narrative elements to strengthen your work.

For instance, Fitzgerald gave Gatsby the tick of incessantly calling people "old sport," an expression of phony camaraderie, with misleading hints of Ivy League superiority. With one detail, Fitzgerald deepened our understanding of a character, and at the same time offered up a leitmotiv ("old sport") that embodied a theme of his book (the falseness that is a result of American ambition). The expression "old sport," then, juggles three narrative aims at once—character definition, leitmotiv, and theme. We cannot, for the sake of analysis, chop a text up into neat, labeled chunks; if we do, we will only get to see one of the many aspects of a phrase. If your reading is rigid, your revision will stop short of itself.

If we choose not to dismember our text, we nonetheless need

a clear road into it. When we read our work (or someone else's), we don't want six narrative ideas to stare back at us at once, creating an impenetrable glare. So I propose a flexible system of reading and analyzing a text. The system depends on two checklists of narrative elements. In keeping with the above thoughts, the separations I have made should never be strictly enforced. Some elements are so naturally linked that I grouped them together.

It is often when we're numb with the fatigue and emotional depletion that writing induces that we edit. In these conditions, we easily forget to address some important aspect of our work. The checklists help us remember, when we're spent, all that we must consider. Eventually we will absorb what's on the lists and won't need to check them. Until rereading thoroughly is second nature, though, you may want to post them at your desk.

These lists aren't exhaustive; they are my personal lay of the land, a tool for finding order when my editing rings out heavy metal in my head instead of Bach.

MACRO-VIEW
1. Intention
2. Character: palpability, credibility, motive
3. Structure: rhythm, tension
4. Foreshadowing
5. Theme: leitmotiv
6. Continuity of tone

MICRO-VIEW
1. Language
2. Repetition
3. Redundancy
4. Clarity
5. Authenticity: image, dialogue
6. Continuity: visuals, character
7. Show and tell
8. Beginnings, endings, transitions

These lists are for writers of any kind. All writers need to ask more or less the same questions of their text. If you are writing a biology treatise, character and motive may or may not apply. But if you are writing a memoir, political or legal history, biography, or novel, they will. It is useful to recall that Ryszard Kapuściński's journalistic account of Haile Selassie in *The Emperor* was as character driven and dramatic as V. S. Naipaul's novel *A Bend in the River* was historically informative. Genres, like rules, are for breaking.

⁓

For those of you who have not read or do not remember *The Great Gatsby*, a synopsis:

It's the 1930s. Nick, a midwesterner, recounts his summer on Long Island, when he rented a small house next to Jay Gatsby's mansion. Nick's cousin, Daisy, lives nearby with her rich, unfaithful husband, Tom. Gatsby, romantic to a degree alternately mystical and pathetic, has a single goal: to reunite with Daisy, whom he'd loved years before. He eventually succeeds; but on learning Gatsby's money was made lawlessly, Daisy breaks off their affair. Immediately after the break, the two drive from Manhattan to Long Island with Daisy at the wheel. A figure steps into the road; Daisy hits it and keeps going. She has unwittingly killed her husband Tom's mistress, Myrtle. Tom convinces Myrtle's husband, Wilson, that Gatsby was the driver. The next day, Wilson mistakenly avenges his wife's death by killing Gatsby.

A discussion of the Macro-View and how it applies to this novel follows.

INTENTION

Intention may be understood as big or small. It is the goal you set for a single aspect of your work: a character you intend as ethereal, an explanation you intend as accessible, an atmosphere you intend as claustrophobic. Intention is also all these aspects combined into your work's overarching aim. Intention, as such, is your central idea that guides both writer and reader. It is your mind's highway that runs clear and wide from the first to last page—while circuitous, pebbly paths lace around it. All other narrative elements (character, leitmotiv, structure, etc.) are the embankment that holds up the road.

Your overall intention will draw the reader with a kind of gravitational force forward and into your written world. If it gets buried in the rubble of the writing process, which is likely, dig your intention out when you edit. You can excavate it by asking yourself: What am I trying to do here? Where am I going with this? You may wish to state your purpose up front (especially in nonfiction) and follow the tradition of expository composition. However, it's often best not to tell your reader what you are doing but to just do it. Stating it up front will not let you off clarity's hook during the rest of your piece. And when you front-load meaning, you destroy the reader's fun in discovering it over time. Better to express your intention throughout your work with varied and subtle means.

Fitzgerald declared his both formal and thematic intentions for *Gatsby* early on. As he embarked on the book, he wrote to Perkins: "in my new novel I'm thrown directly on purely creative work— not trashy imaginings as in my stories but the sustained imagination of a sincere and yet radiant world. . . . This book will be a consciously artistic achievement & must depend on that as the 1st books did not." He set out "to write something new—something

. . . simple & intricately patterned." Fitzgerald used the novel's structure, language, and symbolism to fulfill his intentions. A fluid series of brief, active passages are punctuated by very brief meditations to make the structure "simple." Simple too is the straightforward language. Complexity lies neatly tucked inside *Gatsby's* "intricately patterned" words, actions, and characters.

No one can decide your intention for you. That would be as ludicrous as someone telling you why you want to live. On your own, turn this existential question to your work: Why do you want this piece of writing to live? Your intention lies in how you answer. No answer will be complete, and may you never attempt to explain the authentic mysteries of your writing. But we sometimes claim the safeguarding of art's mystery as permission to write foggy prose; to escape the discipline it takes to understand what we think, what we are doing, and what we want to do.

The intercourse between intention and spontaneity shapes any creative act. We make a plan to more or less control our art, while life's vagaries continually urge us to ignore the plan and let our work respond freely to what's around it. To meander is as crucial as to stay the course. We discover, as we wander, new meanings in our work that we carry back to the narrative highway. It can be hard to know whether, at a given moment, we should stick to our plan or follow a whim. If you veer off the main route, you risk getting lost even as you make important discoveries; if you stay on track, you get where you are going but risk boring the reader with an intention too single-minded and obvious. Ask yourself: Are you wandering in order to stimulate a work that's staid? Or to avoid the apparent tedium of moving straight ahead? In other words, are you being inspired or undisciplined? If it's the latter, force yourself back to the highway.

When you edit others, try to imagine their intention—the terms they set out for themselves, the road they wished to build. If you cannot suss out the writer's intention, then get her on the case. Ask her, what does she mean? Writers may write for a time with no clear intention. Michael Ondaatje (*Anil's Ghost*), for one, writes with a detectivelike curiosity about his own intent, which for a long while eludes him. He doesn't know when he begins what he's after. He discovers his subject and his intention through research and writing. One fragmented image or idea leads to another until several coalesce and he begins to direct them forward. As he starts to direct his fragments into one forward-moving force, his intention surfaces, little by little. It is still surfacing at the editing stage, as Ondaatje tries new things to see what they will yield. At some point, however, he knows the story he wants to tell and maneuvers his material to tell it. Without intention, we can prepare and explore, but we cannot tell a story. Once there is story, there is an intention: a will toward a particular—if supple—end. This drive toward an endpoint does not need to kill spontaneity or intuition. One good example of this comes from pop culture: Eminem as Bunny in the movie *8 Mile* has a clear intention in his climactic battle rap. The rap appears as a moment-to-moment improvisation. Each phrase, though, supports Bunny's intention to expose himself before his opponent can expose him. He intends to tell his own story his own way so that the other guy can't use it against him. This clear intention creates a remarkable quality of inevitability and cohesion.

It is in the editing that a writer clarifies and confirms her intention. You may take a while to know what you really mean. Fine. No hurry. But however difficult it feels to do, before you're done, create a main line for readers to go down in your work.

CHARACTER: PALPABILITY, CREDIBILITY, MOTIVE

*In the course of fashioning a character, you invariably reach
a point where you recognize that you don't know enough
about the person you are trying to create.*

Norman Mailer

In autumn 1924, Max Perkins received the *Gatsby* manuscript
from Fitzgerald and diagnosed its conceptual kinks. In a written
response of formidable clarity, Perkins expressed several concerns,
among them the hero's palpability:

> Among a set of characters marvelously palpable and
> vital—I would know Tom Buchanan if I met him on the
> street and would avoid him—Gatsby is somewhat vague.
> The reader's eyes can never quite focus upon him, his out-
> lines are dim. Now everything about Gatsby is more or less
> a mystery, i.e., more or less vague, and this may be some-
> what of an artistic intention, but I think it is mistaken.

Gatsby's vagueness was intentional according to Fitzgerald's
December 1 reply to Perkins: "[Gatsby's] vagueness I can repair by
making more pointed—this doesn't sound good but wait and see.
It'll make him clear." A vague Gatsby was a mythic one; to make
him too clear would make him too human and unheroic: no
longer a God. Fitzgerald, at this point, wanted to make Gatsby's
"vagueness," not Gatsby himself, clear. However, on December
20 the author wrote again, this time to confess the vagueness was
not altogether intentional:

> *I myself didn't know what Gatsby looked like or was
> engaged in & you felt it. If I'd known & kept it from you you'd*

have been too impressed with my *knowledge to protest.* This is a complicated idea but I'm sure you'll understand. But I know now—and as a penalty for not having known first, in other words to make sure[,] I'm going to tell more.

While Gatsby needed to remain enigmatic, Fitzgerald needed to do as an actor: learn a character's whole history to show only a small piece of it. An actor may explore her character's family tree: Who were my grandmother, father, and sister and how did they treat me? When did I move from city to country and how did the move affect me? On stage the audience may never know Grandma or Sis, or see the countryside or know the trauma that moving there ignited; but if the actor knows, the audience will feel the knowledge as human depth and texture.

Writing teachers like to say a story is in the details. But it is not only in the details revealed, but in those left unsaid that we learn about a person. Just as it is not the telling of our past so much as how it infuses our behavior that expresses who we are. We are encoded; precise experiences metamorphose into a look in the eye, a particular gait, a color worn often, a rhythm of speech, a facial tic, a slumped or upright posture. Gatsby's mysterious persona had to suggest something precise behind it, and Fitzgerald had to figure out what that was. Only then could he figure out the fictional shorthand to represent it.

Consider keeping a notebook for character development. Make entries throughout the writing process, and refer back to them when you edit. Especially for fiction, but also for creative memoir, you might keep a separate notebook for each character, and divide it into two parts: (1) family history and (2) voice. Part two would be used to record bits of dialogue or monologue, where your character speaks to various situations. Carry this book around and try to imagine your character responding to your own experiences her or his way, not yours. When you edit, look through this notebook for a phrase or situation to drop into your text.

Fitzgerald used two techniques during the editing process to discover the full expanse of Gatsby's character: real-life models and visual aids. In a letter to Perkins, he wrote that "after careful searching of the files (of a man's mind here) for the Fuller McGee case and after having had Zelda draw pictures until her fingers ache I know Gatsby better than I know my own child. . . . Gatsby sticks in my heart. I had him for awhile then lost him & now I know I have him again."

The writer had modeled Gatsby on his neighbor in Great Neck, Edward Fuller, who was convicted, with his brokerage firm partner Harold McGee, of fraudulent stock dealing. Fuller was lieutenant to New York racketeer Arnold Rothstein, who was, in turn, the real-life inspiration for Gatsby's boss, Meyer Wolfsheim. Gatsby, according to the author, started out as Fuller and changed into Fitzgerald. When pressed to develop Gatsby, Fitzgerald went back to the idea of Fuller, and set out to learn more about his model's real-life crimes and attitudes.

The old nut goes, write what you know, but often a writer is clearer about what she doesn't know and must learn about. One gets all too easily lost in oneself. The detached concentration that research demanded may have helped Fitzgerald see Gatsby more clearly.

Besides research, the writer used visual imagery to literally flesh out his hero. Zelda, Fitzgerald's artist wife, made drawings of Gatsby, which made him more tangible to his creator. If a character feels muddy and we cannot make her clear, we could go to a museum, open an art book, look at postcards, or sketch until we find a face that fits her. We might do the same to envision a landscape. But beware: Visual aids may trap a writer into inventing less freely. Use an image that helps you see further into your work. If the image constricts your view, let it go.

Zelda's drawings must have helped Fitzgerald, for after spending time with them, he added several physical descriptions of Gatsby. Among them: "His tanned skin was drawn attractively tight on his face and his short hair looked as though it were trimmed every day." This is a good deal better than the original, ultimately and thankfully excised, description of Gatsby, chock-full of generic adjectives and adverbs: "He was undoubtedly one of the handsomest men I had ever seen—the dark blue eyes opening out into lashes of shiny jet were arresting and unforgettable."

After reading Perkins's critique, doing the Fuller research, and staring at Zelda's drawings, Fitzgerald came up with this extraordinary description of Gatsby's smile.

He smiled understandingly—much more than understandingly. It was one of those rare smiles with a quality of eternal reassurance in it, that you may come across four or five times in life. It faced—or seemed to face—the whole external world for an instant, and then concentrated on you with an irresistible prejudice in your favor. It understood you just as far as you wanted to be understood, believed in you as you would like to believe in yourself, and assured you that it had precisely the impression of you that, at your best, you hoped to convey. Precisely at that point it vanished—and I was looking at an elegant young roughneck, a year or two over thirty, whose elaborate formality of speech just missed being absurd.

Fitzgerald wasn't satisfied just to make Gatsby more physical. With one smile, he exposed the entire range of Gatsby's character: the sincerity and generosity of the man who would tragically flip on a dime into blankness and self-absorption.

Sometimes a smile is just a smile. If we try to conjure deep meaning at every turn we will not only sound pretentious, we'll deflect the reader. Nonetheless, Fitzgerald shows us that a mere physical trait can be a porthole to a character's heart. Such a trait must sometimes be added at the end, after the manuscript is done, when the writer can see clearly what is missing and what will best fit into the whole. It would be fair to say that Jay Gatsby was edited, not simply written, into a physical presence.

Even as Fitzgerald worked to better define Gatsby, he took pains to preserve his mysteriousness by fiddling with his voice. In an early manuscript, for example, Nick reported Gatsby's early career to the reader. Later, in unrevised galleys, Gatsby himself told about his past. Later still, in revised galleys, Nick took over again and would remain the teller of Gatsby's past. To what effect? Matthew Bruccoli concludes, "Obviously, he was undecided about how much of the spotlight to put on Gatsby. The effect of the third-person biographical form is to strengthen Nick as narrator and to obscure Gatsby's voice." In other words, in the edit the author realized that a person who talks is more exposed than if talked about. Our voice, the manner in which we speak, gives us away. By keeping Gatsby's voice to a minimum, not just in this scene but throughout the book, the writer enhanced his hero's mystery.

Fitzgerald, it bears noting, obliged his editor without defensiveness. It is easier no doubt to listen to editorial advice when you have taken your book very far on your own. Fitzgerald had edited himself so extensively that by the time Perkins got to it, the *Gatsby* manuscript was almost clean. Perkins only took issue with one structural flaw (which we'll get to), Gatsby's character, and the book's title. (In response to *Among the Ash-Heaps and Millionaires*, Perkins, with his usual courtliness and cogency said, "I do like the idea you have tried to express. The weakness is in the words 'Ash Heap,' which do not seem to me to be a sufficiently definite and concrete expression of that part of the idea." He recommended the writer keep the title he'd once tried a short time back: *The Great Gatsby*. Fitzgerald would go from bad to worse with *Trimalchio in West Egg* before Perkins prevailed.) Fitzgerald was ready for the last editorial push—one he knew he was incapable of envisioning alone. If a good professional edit pisses us off, it's usually because we're angry at ourselves, not our editor, for stopping short on our own before collapsing into another's editorial arms.

It helps, of course, to have an editor as unaggressive and astute as Perkins. To turn the phrase "old sport" into a leitmotiv, for example, was Perkins's idea: "Couldn't [Gatsby] be physically described as distinctly as the others, and couldn't you add one or two characteristics like the use of that phrase 'old sport,'—verbal, but physical ones, perhaps."

Fitzgerald had used the phrase "old sport" only four times when Perkins saw how, used repeatedly, it could sharpen Gatsby's character. Fitzgerald ran with Perkins's idea. In the revised proof, Jay Gatsby says "old sport" incessantly, displaying an absurd, if endearing, self-consciousness. Perkins gave precise suggestions, but preferred to be a dowser indicating the spot where the writer should dig. His call for a more physically defined Gatsby, for instance, stopped there: Fitzgerald responded with the specifics—the smile, tan, and taut skin. A typical Perkins editorial comment was: "I don't know how to suggest a remedy. I hardly doubt that you will find one." Or, "Couldn't Gatsby be . . . and couldn't you add . . . perhaps . . . ?" He was incapable of shoving a good idea down a writer's throat. His light touch led Fitzgerald to acknowledge his editor's "tremendous squareness, courtesy, generosity, and open-mindedness." Perkins's treatment begs the question: Couldn't you be as square, courteous, generous, and open-minded to yourself when you edit your work?

Perkins continued his critique of Gatsby by pointing out that he was less than credible. The reader, Perkins believed, would need some sort of explanation for Gatsby's wealth:

> [Gatsby's] career must remain mysterious, of course. . . . Now almost all readers numerically are going to be puzzled by his having all this wealth and are going to feel entitled to an explanation. To give a distinct and definite one would be, of course, utterly absurd. It did occur to me though, that you might here and there interpolate some phrases, and possibly incidents, little touches of various kinds, that would suggest that he was in some active way mysteriously engaged . . . couldn't he be seen once or twice consulting at his parties with people of some sort of mysterious significance, from the political, the gambling, the sporting world, or whatever it may be. . . . The *total* lack of an explanation through so large a part of the story does seem to me a defect; or not of an explanation, but of the suggestion of an explanation. . . . What Gatsby did ought never to be definitely imparted, even if it could be. . . . But if some sort of

business activity of his were simply adumbrated, it would lend further probability to that part of the story.

Fitzgerald implemented every one of Perkins's suggestions. He added information about Gatsby's past and present profiteering as deftly as a fly fisherman casting his line. Gatsby receives a phone call at a party: " 'Philadelphia wants you on the 'phone, sir.' " Something is going on, but the reader is not sure what. Following his editor's cue, Fitzgerald hints more loudly as the story progresses. In the following passage, added in the edit, Nick recounts how skittish Gatsby is about his illicit business affairs:

> . . . when I asked him what business he was in he answered: "That's my affair," before he realized that it wasn't an appropriate reply. "Oh, I've been in several things," he corrected himself. "I was in the drug business and then I was in the oil business. But I'm not in either one now . . ."

In another added passage, Gatsby proposes that Nick get involved in stock fraud, though the term is cleverly omitted:

> "—you see I carry on a little business on the side, a sort of side line, you understand. And I thought that if you don't make very much—You're selling bonds, aren't you, old sport? . . . Well, . . . It wouldn't take up much of your time and you might pick up a nice bit of money. It happens to be a rather confidential sort of thing."

What lay behind Gatsby's wealth was, then, as Perkins had hoped, "simply adumbrated."

Fitzgerald uncovered Gatsby so gently, folded his crimes into his glories so delicately, that we do not at first anticipate his downfall, and we are loath to morally judge him. He remains defined not by dark deeds but luminous aspirations. Gatsby was in a hurry to rise above the fray, and to him, as scholar Richard Lehan writes, "money is money, and he never understands the difference between . . . the established wealth [and] . . . the new rich or, like himself, the ersatz and criminally rich." Gatsby, both godly and childlike, was beyond distinctions of high and low, of wealth that was criminal or noble—indeed, noble wealth, as Lehan points out, was originally criminal before it got cleansed by countless years in banks and posh real estate. Fitzgerald was well aware of this irony. *The Great Gatsby*, then, indicts society for the simplemindedness with which it judges its members. Gatsby is too complex and lovable to be so easily condemned.

In order to make Gatsby an outlaw that readers would feel tender toward, Fitzgerald kept reworking Gatsby's criminal side. In an early version, Tom claimed Gatsby had been squeezing money out of "taxi drivers and drunks and the poor bums that hang around the streets." Fitzgerald realized this brutal racket would make Gatsby too unsympathetic, and eased off. As he edited the proof, he wrote to Perkins: "hold up the galley of Chapter X. The correction—and God! It's important because in my other revision I made Gatsby look too mean—is enclosed herewith." Gatsby ended up in bootlegging, which in the 1920s was considered a service to society more than a nasty crime. Gambling and stolen securities—mere white-collar missteps—were his other line of "work." Gatsby was unquestionably naughty, but relatively harmless. Through ardent editing, Fitzgerald tuned him to the perfect criminal pitch.

So say you've made your character's economic and social status credible, you've made her physically palpable, and given her behavioral tics that represent her state of mind. Still, with all that, she isn't coming clear, doesn't slip off the page and into your life. If it isn't time to ditch her, it's time to work on her motive. To test a character's motive, ask yourself: What is it that she really wants? Motive, in this context, means raison d'être, a reason for getting out of bed each morning to face the day. Every character needs one. Go back and create a motive for any character who feels flat; if her motive is recognizable but weak, strengthen it.

What is it that Gatsby really wants? Fitzgerald didn't need help on this one. He knew what made his hero want to get out of bed every day. It was simple (or seemed to be): Gatsby existed to fulfill his dream of winning back Daisy.

The less obvious answer is naturally more profound. Daisy was the "nice girl" that soldier Jimmy Gatz, who by now called himself Jay Gatsby, fell in love with on leave. He was, not insignificantly, in a soldier's uniform that hid his unpedigreed background when he met Daisy, whose niceness derived from her family's wealth as much as her enchanting demeanor—"her voice is full of money," Gatsby would later tell Nick. The memory of her motivates him to get rich to win her back. But long before she entered his life, Gatsby was motivated to rise out of mediocrity: "Jimmy was bound to get ahead," his father says after Gatsby's death. He has shown Nick a notebook he came across marked "schedule and general resolves." Included in the list written eleven years before meeting Daisy, when Gatsby was only a boy, are "Practice elocution, poise and how to attain it . . . Read one improving book or magazine per week . . . Save $5.00 [crossed out] $3.00 per week." His father remarks: "He always had some resolves like this or something. Do you notice what he's got about improving his mind? He was always great for that. He told me I et like a hog once and I beat him for it." It was, at bottom, not Daisy, but the all-American dream of a better, more glorious life that motivated Gatsby. Daisy was a symbol of that life and a handle on it. If Gatsby could grab on to her, she would pull him up into a higher realm.

Fitzgerald feared, even after publication, that he had never found a motive sufficient to justify Daisy's actions in the book. Earlier, when he had told Perkins that he now knew Gatsby better than he knew his own child, he had also written, "I'm sorry Myrtle [Tom's mistress] is better than Daisy." Then, in the spring of 1925, after the novel's commercial thud, he wrote to Edmund Wilson, "I was awfully happy that you like it [*Gatsby*] and that you approved of the design. The worst fault in it, I think is a BIG FAULT: I gave no account (and had no feeling or knowledge of) the emotional relations between Gatsby and Daisy from the time of their reunion to the catastrophe."

And to Mencken, he wrote: "There is a tremendous fault in the book—the lack of an emotional presentment of Daisy's attitude toward Gatsby after their reunion (and the consequent lack of logic or importance in her throwing him over)."

Motive is so essential that if Daisy hadn't been given enough, the book failed. The book did fail commercially, and in some circles, critically as well.

Fitzgerald had edited the book so meticulously, now he searched for a flaw to explain its downfall. All he could come up with was Daisy, and her undeveloped love and rejection of Gatsby. But the writer, in his despair, may have mistaken the limitations of Daisy's and Gatsby's intimacy for Daisy's limits as a character.

Daisy is distant from the reader because she is distant period. Ravishing, charismatic, and clever, she is missing some quality that would deepen her sense of consequence in the world and allow her to truly connect to others and grow. She was sketchy by nature, not Fitzgerald's lax hand.

To test Daisy's credibility, we need to ask: What is it that Daisy really wants? Answer: adoration and security; to be surrounded by beautiful things that confirm her own beauty—a beauty that depends on wealth to keep its sheen; and which is, by definition, static: the opposite of decay, the opposite of death. What Daisy wants, at bottom, is the immortality that beauty signifies. She betrayed Gatsby at the Plaza because his dirty money was unreliable. A criminal might end up in jail and leave her penniless, scruffy, mortal. With her raison d'être to outwit death with money, it was perfectly logical for her to jilt Gatsby. Fitzgerald had given Daisy a motive and actions that were its logical outcome; he had, without knowing it, made her complete and convincing.

To look closer at Fitzgerald's edit is to see just how far he went with Daisy. Her inability to grow up (i.e., her effort at immortality), for instance, is stitched into two scenes. In chapter four, Nick arrives to find Daisy and her friend Jordan lying on a couch in the excruciating heat of the day. Referring to the torpor, the women say simultaneously, "We can't move." After this scene was written, at the stage of a galley proof, Fitzgerald returned to chapter one to sew in a prescient phrase: on seeing Nick for the first time in years, Daisy says, "I'm p-paralyzed with happiness." Daisy's inability to move in chapter four reverberates with her paralysis in chapter one. An inability to move defines Daisy. It defines her actions (jilting Gatsby, staying with Tom) and inactions (not going back to check on the person she drove into, not sending condolences to Gatsby's funeral). She wants only to stay still—untouched by degradation and death.

A character's motive can bulge through the text, like Gatsby's; or, like Daisy's, lie smoothly embedded in it. If the reader sees or feels it, the character is working. If not, you need to reexamine the foundation on which your character is built. Give your character a reason to rise each day—and if she is so depressed she can't rise, then give her a reason to stay in bed. Ask: What does she really want?

During the revision, Fitzgerald was still learning who some of his characters were. It is a common error to think editing simply means to replace poorly written phrases with new, better-turned ones. Editing can, and often will, mean to rethink a character, research her further until your understanding, not just your language, is new. Editing can also mean patterning events, dialogue, or imagery to solidify a character's gestalt—just as Fitzgerald did when he returned to the first chapter to link Daisy's dialogue there to her dialogue in a later chapter. From Fitzgerald let us learn not to be lazy or shortsighted. Fatigue can make us so. Get some rest. Then open up the old files, maybe make new ones, and embroider backward even in the last revisionist hours.

STRUCTURE: RHYTHM, TENSION

Max, it amuses me when praise comes in on the "structure" of the book—because it was you who fixed up the structure, not me. And don't think I'm not grateful for all that sane and helpful advice about it.

F. Scott Fitzgerald

Structure is the design that underpins your prose. It is your narrative fence. Without it, your words scamper about like an unruly flock of sheep—impossible to follow. A functioning structure guides readers from one idea or incident to the next without their stopping to wonder where they are and where they are going.

Structural imbalance makes itself known by, as Perkins put it, "sagging": where the narrative drags instead of trots along. This does not mean every paragraph must enthrall by some action or suspense. An idea or image alone, if stylistically honed, can interest a reader for large portions of a work (think of Robert Musil's philosophical narrative in *The Man Without Qualities* or Virginia Woolf's extended imagery in most everything she wrote). You should be able to discern, though, the difference between the ruminative and the downright, unalterably boring. If a portion of your text is boring, figure out what is amiss. Maybe there is uninteresting material, fatty sentences, or redundancies that need cutting; but structure may be the less overt problem. Ask yourself if you have organized your material to best fulfill its purpose.

If you want to write a freewheeling, unstructured stream of consciousness, okay, but beware: your language will have to be brilliantly muscular and locomotive to create the tension and propulsion necessary to move a reader forward—a tension and propulsion normally created from structure as much as words. Elizabeth Smart, for instance, achieves great tension and drive in her compressed lyric *By Grand Central Station I Sat Down and Wept*. As do Michael Ondaatje in *Coming Through Slaughter* and W. G. Sebald in *The Rings of Saturn*. The structures in these works are far less prominent than the language. Structure is not abandoned so much as distilled into careful collage and juxtaposition. A distilled structure offers a highly subtle support and driving mechanism that needs combustible or, at the least, meaningful wordplay to move a reader from one page to the next.

Many, if not most, writers forgo poetic collage for a more architectonic approach. Editing structure of any kind can be overwhelming. This is because it can be extremely difficult to see a structure that has become hidden by the incidents, characters, and concepts that constitute story. Just as we cannot detect the underpainting on a canvas that has been painted over with its final imagery, we literally cannot find the structure under our essay or story. If we cannot find it, we cannot correct it.

The only way to improve our ability to see structure is to look harder at it, in our own work and in others'. When you read a book you love, force your mind to see its contours. Concentrate on structure without flinching until it reveals itself. Text is a plastic art, not just a verbal one: it has a shape. To train your mind to see shapes more easily, write them (and sketch them if you like) in a notebook. As with writing down dreams, the more you write, the more you will see. The structure notebook will be a bank of ideas and enhancements when you edit. It is probably better to avoid filching whole hog somebody else's structure. Let yours grow out of your own material. Jay Gatsby is dead, for instance, as the story unfolds, which naturally calls forth an elegy: a narrative shaped in short Bible-like passages, punctuated by Nick's sermons (meditations on society, immorality, and temptation).

Here are some examples of narrative shapes to jog your visual mind. The easiest to see is a linear, chronological line that draws a story from start to middle to end. However, strict linear chronology may be the most plodding, insipid structure of all. A cardiogram-esque zigzag would include flashbacks and flashforwards. A narrative river might have contemplative eddies at regular intervals (*The Great Gatsby*). Maybe you've divided your story into three sections, or two or seven, that resemble stacking blocks; maybe an arc begins narrow—to carry a single idea and event along—then widens at the apex, where several ideas and events spread out, then narrows again to the original single idea and event—resembling the shape of a wristwatch. Some structural designs have a few climaxes, some only one. Most, however, do well to have a degree of balance and elegant proportion.

A vivid example of a structure custom-built for its inhabitants is found in John Hawkes's exquisite novella *Travesty*. *Travesty*'s story line is simple: a man called Papa drives two passengers—his daughter, Chantal, and his best friend, Henri—to their deaths (a murder and suicide in one). The telling of the story, however, is anything but simple. To start with, Hawkes devised severe constraints for himself: the entire story occurs inside a car, while only one voice, Papa's, ever speaks. Startlingly, this single-setting monologue—a recipe for monotony—grips the reader's attention so tightly that one still feels the pressure years after reading it. Here's a taste of this brutal masterpiece, where Papa addresses Henri, a famous poet, about Honorine—the former's wife, the latter's mistress:

> But what of all those first days and months and seasons when I retired early to my own sumptuous but monastic room, took unnecessary business trips, bundled Chantal off to mountain holidays? Have you forgotten how considerate I was, and how discreet, ingenious, flattering? Don't you remember Honorine's pleasure when there were two gifts of flowers on the piano in a single day? Or all those winter evenings when, on the white leather divan, the three of us enjoyed together the portfolio of large, clear photographs depicting the charming pornographic poses of a

most intelligent woman of good birth? Surely you remember that visual history of the life of Honorine from youth to middle age in which her own appreciation of her piquant autoeroticism becomes increasingly subtle, increasingly bold? Surely you will not have forgotten the night when you remarked that every man hopes for an ordinary wife who will prove a natural actress in the theater of sex? Well, I savored that remark for days. I still do. It was perhaps the only poetic remark you ever made.

How did Hawkes keep a one-scene, one-voice novella going? We could credit his inimitable gift for language and extraordinary psychological, moral, and philosophical insights. But we shouldn't ignore the importance of *Travesty*'s unusual structure. Hawkes rejected the narrative convention of an introduction, acceleration, climax, and denouement. Instead, he shaped his story like a cone: wide open at the front, and spiraling inward toward a black hole. He kicked the climactic revelation and denouement up front so the reader immediately discovers, on the first page no less, that everyone in the car will die soon, and that Henri has seduced Papa's daughter: "Not many young women have the opportunity of passing their last minutes in the company of lover and loving Papa both." Before the second page is done, we learn Henri has seduced Papa's wife as well. A whodunit this is not. Acceleration is irrelevant, because the story, like its narrator, speeds from start to finish—"you will not believe it," Papa says meaningfully in the book's opening paragraph, "but we are still accelerating." There are further revelations about the characters and their relationships, but they do not constitute a climax, just a deepening intimacy with the reader. The crash would have been the climax, but Hawkes refuses us such cheap satisfaction—we never see it. Tantric sex explains what Hawkes is doing better than any literary or academic model: foreplay takes over and continues for so long that climax is no longer the point. It is the driver's psychological stimulation of his passengers that engages us; until not climax but depletion sets in, death instead of pleasure. Tantrism here begets nihilism. The narrative cone has narrowed and closed to a point of near total darkness—not total because we are spared the crash itself. This narrative pinhole of light at the end perhaps signals a kind of ruthless redemption.

⌒

Some writers ignore structure at the start of a project, and gradually coax it out of their material. Some—in particular, traditional nonfiction writers—need a design before they begin, which they edit along their way, as unforeseen twists in their material make new demands. If you have trouble with structure, it may be helpful to choose one straight off and use it as a guardrail as you write. You may need to replace it later, as your writing spills out of your plan, but you will have learned a lot about the meaning of structure by forcing yourself to conceive of one at the start. It can be easier to find the right one by butting up against a wrong one than against nothing at all.

More than a few of us worry that our structure will prove, at the stage of editing, altogether misbegotten. We fear we will have to demolish it, and the prospect of reconstruction from scratch devastates. It feels as if a tremendous amount of work we did was a waste of time. This is never so, however. In writing out those pages, our thoughts and craft matured; this new maturity will enhance our next draft. "Much of what I wrote last summer," Fitzgerald once told Perkins, "was good but it was so interrupted that it was jagged + in approaching it from a new angle I've had to discard a lot of it—in one case 18,000 words." I doubt Fitzgerald celebrated the need to rewrite eighteen thousand words, but he wrote them, and from all evidence, wrote them better.

More often than not, though, you'll need to reconceive certain parts of your text and simply rearrange them. Rather than a razing, your work will probably need selective rebuilding. You must gingerly select what's dispensable, what's superb, what can be opened up and tinkered with, and what is too fragile to touch.

In *Gatsby*, for example, Fitzgerald discovered a tedious section but could not understand what was wrong. Perkins did. A clump of undramatic biographical information about Gatsby had been expediently shoved into one place, and Perkins knew this clumping was deadly. He said as much to Fitzgerald, in his characteristically gallant manner: "In giving deliberately Gatsby's biography when he gives it to the narrator, you do depart from the method of the narrative in some degree, for otherwise almost everything is told, and beautifully told, in the regular flow of it,—in the succession of events in accompaniment with time."

Perkins wanted biographical information told dramatically, not as an informational aside. Actors have an expression for the mere facts an audience must know to understand a story—they call them the plumbing. "I'm not doing the plumbing," some will protest, when asked to say a few lines that explain plot or character history but stick out from the action. Similarly, the plumbing of a novel must not stick out. At its best, a book's pipes are laid into the work so suavely that the reader will not notice them function.

Perkins wanted Fitzgerald to dole out historical details about

Gatsby and integrate them into the action. In talking the problem through with his writer, the editor helped him reconceive data as drama: "I think you are right in feeling a certain slight sagging in chapters six and seven . . . I thought you might find ways to let the truth of some of his claims like 'Oxford' and his army career come out bit by bit in the course of actual narrative."

The main problem was the scene where Nick goes over to Gatsby's house after the fatal car accident. The two men go to the terrace and sit "smoking out into the summer night." Into this static setting Gatsby tells his life story. "Suddenly he was telling me a lot of things," Nick says. He may as well have said, Warning: the next few paragraphs are hazardous to your attention span. You are about to be blanketed with "a lot of" data. Soon, Fitzgerald would delete Nick's warning, just as he would pull apart, redistribute, pare down, and partially reword the entire scene.

In the early version, Gatsby had a chat with Nick during which he explained his Oxford claim, then recounted his teenage reveries and his subsequent apprenticeship with yachtsman Dan Cody from which followed his army career during which he met and fell in love with Daisy Fay, after which he received a letter at Oxford telling him he had lost her to Tom Buchanan. Are you with me? I wouldn't blame you if you weren't. Clumping does not work. We lose interest in the monotonous rhythm of a history recounted in one, unchanging voice. Dramatic tension fizzles the more Gatsby tells and doesn't show; it fizzles from too much important information coming out too fast, which decimates the reader's sense of peeling back the layers of a mystery. Finally, the sudden change of tone annoys: the literary ballet has suddenly become an infommercial.

To see how dramatically different a draft can be from a finished work, read the original manuscript version of this scene right before you read the published version (see below). A flat recitation has transformed, through editing, into a dynamic, gradual disclosure. How did Fitzgerald revise his way out of this biographical thicket? He cut Gatsby's biography into small pieces and judiciously distributed them throughout the text. He folded most of them into dialogue and drama. The Plaza confrontation scene (which comes one chapter before Nick and Gatsby sit and smoke "out into the summer night") originally carried no reference to Gatsby's Oxford claim or his army career; in the revised proof, Fitzgerald fully explains and seamlessly weaves the Oxford and army stories into the scene's drama.

Original version:

> . . . suddenly Tom was quarreling violently with Gatsby over [Daisy's] emotions.
>
> "Be quiet, Tom," said Daisy a little frightened, "There're people here. That Mrs. Rolf from Hemstead is here—"
>
> Tom kept looking at Gatsby. "What kind of row are you trying to cause in my house anyhow?"
>
> "He isn't causing any row," whispered Daisy tensely, "You're causing a row. Please have a little self controll."
>
> "Self controll!" repeated Tom incredulously, "Self controll! . . . "Who the devil are you anyway?"
>
> Gatsby looked at Daisy as if seeking permission to reply.
>
> "You're one of that bunch that hangs around Myer Wolfshiem," went on Tom, "That much I happen to know."

Daisy got up from the table. "Come on. Let's go home."

"All right," agreed Tom, "but I want your friend here to realize that his little flirtation is over."

Published version:

Gatsby's foot beat a short, restless tattoo and Tom eyed him suddenly. "By the way, Mr. Gatsby, I understand you're an Oxford man."

"Not exactly."

"Oh, yes, I understand you went to Oxford."

"Yes—I went there."

A pause. Then Tom's voice, incredulous and insulting: "You must have gone there about the time Biloxi [a poseur who'd falsely claimed he'd gone to Yale] went to New Haven."

Another pause. A waiter knocked and came in with crushed mint and ice but the silence was unbroken by his "Thank you" and the soft closing of the door. This tremendous detail was to be cleared up at last.

"I told you I went there," said Gatsby.

"I heard you, but I'd like to know when."

"It was in nineteen-nineteen. I only stayed five months. That's why I can't really call myself an Oxford man."

Tom glanced around to see if we mirrored his unbelief. But we were all looking at Gatsby.

"It was an opportunity they gave to some of the officers after the Armistice," he continued. "We could go to any of the universities in England or France."

I wanted to get up and slap him on the back. I had one of those renewals of complete faith in him that I'd experienced before.

Daisy rose, smiling faintly, and went to the table. "Open the whiskey, Tom," she ordered. "And I'll make you a mint julep. Then you won't seem so stupid to yourself. . . ."

"Wait a minute," snapped Tom. "I want to ask Mr. Gatsby one more question."

"Go on," Gatsby said politely.

"What kind of row are you trying to cause in my house anyhow?"

It is hard to imagine a writer revising his work with sharper aim. Precisely as Perkins had hoped, Fitzgerald made Gatsby's "claims like 'Oxford' and his army career come out bit by bit in the course of actual narrative."

One particular design in *Gatsby* should not go unnoted. Fitzgerald structured the first three chapters to advertise the book's central theme of class—a theme confirmed by the book's original title, *Among the Ash Heaps and Millionaires.* (That title confirms, as well, just how off someone so on can be.) At the end of chapter three, Nick calls attention to a trio of nights spent out: "Reading over what I have written so far, I see I have given the impression that the events of three nights several weeks apart were all that absorbed me. On the contrary, they were merely casual events in a crowded summer."

Simply by mentioning them, Nick slyly throws a spotlight on the far-from-casual "three nights." Each night, one for each of the first three chapters, gives the reader a bird's-eye view of a different social class: the old rich, the poor, and the new rich. The first three chapters create a tripod, then, on which sits the rest of the novel. Fitzgerald did not achieve this effect right off the bat. A lot of chapter shifting led up to it. Chapters one and two were written first. But later, the author pushed chapter two forward to become chapter three. Later still, he wrote and inserted the book's final chapter two. At last, after much editing, he had it: three social classes set into place, compressed and ready to combust.

Here is a sampling of the three chapters/three nights that antagonize one another and yet, together, state one coherent theme:

Chapter one: Nick dines at Tom and Daisy's, joined by Jordan Baker. The evening is a bland exercise in aristocratic indolence:

> Sometimes [Daisy] and Miss Baker talked at once, unobtrusively and with a bantering inconsequence that was never quite chatter, that was as cool as their white dresses and their impersonal eyes in the absence of all desire.

Chapter two: Nick attends a party at Myrtle Wilson's—Tom's proletariat mistress. The party is a model of earthy pleasures, vulgar speech, and crass pretension.

> "My dear," [Myrtle] told her sister in a high, mincing shout, "most of these fellas will cheat you every time. All they think of is money. I had a woman up here last week to look at my feet, and when she gave me the bill you'd of thought she had my appendicitis out."

Chapter three: Nick goes to his first Gatsby shindig—a preposterously sumptuous affair filled with famous people and ironic repartee, a showcase for nouveau riche opportunism:

I was immediately struck by the number of young En-
glishmen dotted about; all . . . talking in low, earnest voices
to solid, prosperous Americans. I was sure that they were
selling something: bonds or insurance or automobiles.
They were at least agonizingly aware of the easy money in
the vicinity and convinced that it was theirs for a few words
in the right key.

These three excerpts emit the high, low, and middle register of
one chime—that of human nature. We learn, in what amounts to
a prologue, that all these dramatically different people are, at
heart, the same. Fitzgerald's is a dismally democratic view. Vanity
is the human disease everybody shares, no matter what their social
standing—and it drives them all on a collision course with fate.
Only Nick, the writer, Fitzgerald's doppelgänger, is somewhat
exempted—the outsider who moves in and out of all three classes.

Structure, then, is not a straitjacket for your words. It is an
architecture that moves readers through and allows them to
pause, not randomly, but with direction.

⌐⌐

When you reread, listen for "sagging." Listen for whether or
not your ideas sound organized or scattershot. Saggy or scattered
writing usually means you are not directing your reader well
enough, not creating a clear road for her to take. For immediate,
total, and continual clarity, follow the old rule of stating your the-
sis, explaining and proving it, then summarizing it, perhaps with
a philosophical curl at the end. But not all essays, memoir, or
biography will want this structural formula applied. Nonfiction

holds as much imaginative structural possibility as fiction. Take John D'Agata's essay on Edvard Munch's painting *The Scream* (from his book *The Lifespan of a Fact*). The first two-thirds do not mention the artist or the painting, but instead talk about a nuclear waste depot and the eclectic group assembled to determine the signage it should bear for the next ten thousand years. The essay goes backward, reaching its beginning at the end, when Munch's personal life and motives for making the famous painting (to be hung at the nuclear waste site) are examined. The unorthodox structure makes the reader question what the essay is really about; it suggests that any one topic sits, iceberglike, as the mere tip of a hidden mass of topics below. Or consider Tracy Kidder's account of the quest to build the "perfect computer" in the 1970s. *The Soul of a New Machine* won the Pulitzer Prize presumably not because it was informative and clear, but because, with its first chapter set on a boat in a storm, it was structured to have the narrative ferocity, character richness, and mystery of a novel.

With any kind of writing, try to name or draw its form if it helps you to grasp it better. Do not, however, preoccupy yourself with making fancy, formulaic diagrams that will stifle more than free you. Whether you need to reconfigure your lyric corridors or redesign the whole house, do not shy away from editing structure.

FORESHADOWING

A staple of the so-called page-turner, foreshadowing plants your text with signals of what's ahead and heightens your reader's curiosity. And while mystery writers have laid claim to the classic page-turner, writers of every kind want to write one. What writer, after all, doesn't want her reader to eagerly turn the page? At the heart of our desire to read on is the desire to discover—a law of physics, who will sleep with whom, how a man will keep his dignity as he dies, if hybrid corn will hurt the environment, how the impressionists influenced the cubists. Whether we are science writers, children's writers, or art critics, we have to compel readers to the end. Foreshadowing is a good tool for it, and editing is an ideal time to introduce and hone your foreshadowing.

It was not until galleys, for instance, that Fitzgerald added a conversation at Myrtle's party about Gatsby to chapter two, so we would hear about him just before we'd meet him for the first time in chapter three. "Do you know him?" someone says to Nick. ". . . Well, they say he's a nephew of Kaiser Wilhelm's. That's where all his money comes from. . . . I'm scared of him. I'd hate to have him get anything on me." By having someone speculate on Gatsby early on, Fitzgerald piques our interest in him, even as he sets Gatsby up as mysterious and threatening.

Foreshadowing can work in both obvious and subtle incarnations. If a reader feels like a huge mechanical hand has lifted her up and moved her from point A to point B, it's a good bet the foreshadowing is too obvious. In Nick's prologue, Fitzgerald's obvious signals are delicately implanted in sentences that are as much about character as momentum. Our deepening knowledge of Nick distracts us so we don't think too hard about the alert coming across the wire.

> When I came back from the East last autumn I felt that
> I wanted the world to be in uniform and at a sort of moral
> attention forever.

Something bad must have happened back East to make Nick feel this insecure and sullied. He goes on to describe Gatsby:

> There was something gorgeous about [Gatsby] . . . it was an extraordinary gift for hope, a romantic readiness such as I have never found in any other person and which it is not likely I shall ever find again. No—Gatsby turned out all right at the end; it is what preyed on Gatsby, what foul dust floated in the wake of his dreams that temporarily closed out my interest in the abortive sorrows and short-winded elations of men.

Nick's despair is a flashing red light: What will happen in this story, we wonder, to destroy his faith in humanity? Fitzgerald gets us to concentrate on the nuance and voltage of Nick's voice even as Nick's foreshadowing message crudely summons us forward. Later, as Nick drives with Gatsby to New York City, he ruminates: "anything can happen now that we've slid over this bridge . . . anything at all." Practically Gothic in tone, Nick's foreboding, we sense, relates not to this particular outing but to some larger, unknown fate. Again, Fitzgerald's characterizations and descriptions are so potent, his bald foreshadowing has an unlikely poise.

The most interesting, and arguably most effective, signals go to the reader's subconscious mind. Accordingly, Fitzgerald used foreshadowing that was, in essence, hidden. He foreshadowed the final, fatal car accident—the book's apotheosis—with a fearless slight of hand. His signals are laughably easy to see once you reach the end and go back, and nearly impossible to recognize as you read the novel for the first time. After Nick's first party at Gatsby's, for instance, a car drives into a ditch and ends up "violently shorn of one wheel." Soon thereafter, Nick says,

> . . . we had a curious conversation about driving a car. It started because she passed so close to some workman that our fender flicked a button on one man's coat.
>
> "You're a rotten driver," I protested. "Either you ought to be more careful, or you oughtn't to drive at all."
>
> "I am careful."
>
> "No, you're not."
>
> "Well, other people are," she said lightly.
>
> "What's that got to do with it?"
>
> "They'll keep out of my way," she insisted. "It takes two to make an accident."
>
> "Suppose you met somebody just as careless as yourself."
>
> "I hope I never will," she answered. "I hate careless people. That's why I like you."

This one short passage harbors the morality play of the entire novel. It presents, as well, a sketch for the final disastrous car accident, wherein Daisy and Myrtle (society's high and low) will be equally careless. Then there is Ripley Snells, who was "so drunk out on the gravel drive that Mrs. Ulysses Swett's automobile ran over his right hand." Finally, at the very beginning of the book a bizarre, morbid reference to cars foreshadows the novel's end. Nick tells Daisy,

> I told her how I had stopped off in Chicago . . . , and how a dozen people had sent their love through me.

"Do they miss me?" she cried ecstatically.

"The whole town is desolate. All the cars have the left rear wheel painted black as a mourning wreath, and there's a persistent wail all night along the north shore."

The magnificently strange image of car wheels as mourning wreaths becomes less strange when understood as a presaging piece of a narrative puzzle. The book's many references to dangerous driving and automobiles in various states of distress are like a silhouette that, with every reference, becomes more full-bodied, until the climactic crash, when at last we see clearly what's before us—and, in a sense, has been from the start.

It is said in feng shui, the ancient Chinese art of making space accommodate the spirit, that you should hang a picture or other tantalizing object on a wall at the end of a corridor that takes a turn. This is because the person walking down it should not face a blank space, but be pulled forth by an intriguing image; this way, she will make it to the end and turn. So it is in writing. Editing is the opportune time to get an overview of your story's proportions, rhythm, and tension. When you reread your draft, look for the walls still left blank at the end of turning corridors, where you may place an arrow, as it were, to get your reader to make the turn.

THEME: LEITMOTIV

Leitmotiv, one of those words that people nod at, then go home to look up in the dictionary, is, according to the *Oxford English Dictionary*, "a recurrent idea or image in a literary work." Leitmotiv, used well, gives a layered depth and resonance to an otherwise stark plot. Used clumsily, it is pedantic. Fitzgerald pushed the device further than one would think it could go. *The*

Great Gatsby is leitmotiv-laden, yet the device feels natural, not pushy. He knew when he crossed the line from beauty to excess. He gets away with so much calculation, too, because his characters affect the reader so, making the book more than an intellectual drill. Most of all, though, Fitzgerald succeeded at his lavish use of leitmotiv because he was a tireless editor, fine-tuning ad infinitum. What follows are some examples of how the final edit, along with the initial writing, gave way to a symbolic pattern.

In Gatsby, light, along with the colors white and green, are leitmotivs that point up the troubled relations between money and purity in modern America. Light, in the novel, represents truth or glitter. It is beatific or blinding: the light of pure love or that of superficial beauty that calls one, like a siren, to the shallow reef. Light, white and green, irradiates most of the novel in contrast to the occasional ashen hue and heaviness of poverty. In the first chapter, for example, when Nick visits Tom and Daisy's home, he notices "the **white** palaces of fashionable East Egg **glittered** along the water"; Tom and Daisy's house had a "line of French windows, **glowing** now with **reflected gold**"; their porch was "**sunny**"; their windows were "**gleaming white**"; Daisy and Jordan, at first sight, "were both in **white**"; Daisy's face "was sad and lovely with **bright** things in it, **bright** eyes and a **bright** passionate mouth"; she looked at her guests "**radiantly**" (boldface added). The suggestion of light is no less meaningful. Daisy says to her guests:

> In two weeks it'll be the longest day in the year. Do you always watch for the longest day of the year and then miss it? I always watch for the longest day in the year and then miss it.

She watches, in other words, for the longest light—light of moral purity and the pure love it brings (note how Fitzgerald foreshadows her doom; if she has always missed it, chances are she always will). In another elliptical reference to light, Nick says of Gatsby's parties, people "came and went like moths."

Yet more light: "for a moment **the last sunshine fell** . . . upon [Daisy's] **glowing** face"; in her house, the "crimson room **bloomed with light**"; and "the **lamp-light, bright** on [Tom's] boots . . . **glinted** along the paper." Once home, Nick watched Gatsby stretch his arms out "toward the water in a curious way . . . he glanced seaward—and distinguished nothing except **a single green light**, minute and far away, that might have been the end of a dock."

In the last stages of editing, Fitzgerald went back to the first chapter to add the green light at the end of Daisy's dock. He linked that green light to the two on the last page: "I thought of Gatsby's wonder when he first picked out the green light at the end of Daisy's dock." And, "Gatsby believed in the green light, the orgiastic future that year by year recedes before us." The green light is more than the color of money and the light of love. It is the universal signal to go that symbolizes Gatsby's having gone forward toward his dream. In a supreme act of patterning, accomplished through editing, Fitzgerald's green lights are dream poles that hold up the span of sad reality that is the book.

To use as much symbolism as Fitzgerald would be impossible for us all to do gracefully, nor would it suit every text. But we should not abstain just because it's strong stuff. Try to gauge what your text can take. Fitzgerald pulled back when he'd gone too far. Before the final edit, Nick's first encounter with Daisy and Jordan read:

They were both in white and their dresses were rippling and fluttering as if they had just blown in after a short flight around the house. I must have stood for a few moments on the threshold, dazzled by the alabaster light, listening to the whip and snap of the curtains and the groan of a picture on the wall.

The same paragraph in the finished book:

They were both in white, and their dresses were rippling and fluttering as if they had just been blown back in after a short flight around the house. I must have stood for a few moments listening to the whip and snap of the curtains and the groan of a picture on the wall.

Fitzgerald likely decided that "dazzled by the alabaster light" would tip the passage over the line.

When you use leitmotiv, remember Raymond Chandler's advice on creating an afterglow: "From the beginning, . . . it was always a question . . . of putting into the stuff something [the public] would not shy off from, perhaps even not know was there as a conscious realization, but which would somehow distill through their minds and leave an afterglow."

A writer may (and generally should) reflect on her symbols, but her audience should not. Not on first read at least. The leitmotiv should gather itself into a polyphony sung so that the reader cannot tease out the individual voices.

Leitmotiv grows out of a theme, or it is gratuitous. You don't want an image of light recurring throughout your story if the idea of light has no bearing on it. Ask yourself then: What are my themes? A theme is not a message. It is an idea written in invisible ink on the backside of your text. Choose a theme you want to emphasize. Then think of what image could represent it. Make it nonliteral—do not dumb down your theme with a cliché, such as rice for the East or corn for the West. Metaphorical symbols, such as color, texture, fragrance, or sound, may work better. A leitmotiv should not speak so much as resonate. A piece of discordant music or a grating noise might signal abrasive communication; velvety surfaces—marshmallows, pussy willows, a stuffed animal, a velvet coat—could signal love's comfort. Bamboo might symbolize flexibility; metal, modernity; the smell of burning, infidelity. Actions can be leitmotivs: lighting a fire, crossing a river, feeding a bird: any of these can evoke specific emotions (enlightenment, forgiveness, generosity, respectively) and add dimension to your text. Maybe a girl who is gaining enlightenment keeps walking across things, getting from one place to another—a bridge, a ladder, a plank set over a puddle. But if she performs the same action too many times, your subtle hint will slap too hard on the reader's head. (For a further example and discussion of leitmotiv, see "An Editing Collaboration in the Corporate World" in chapter five.)

It is in editing that you can best see the symbolic pattern you've wrought. As with foreshadowing, hang your entire text on a clothesline or lay it on the floor to help you view the lacework of imagery. You might highlight the leitmotivs with a marker to see where too many cluster in one area, not enough in another. Quantity is not the only issue. Read through your draft to make sure every symbolic image integrates into your text, and does not sit on top as decoration.

CONTINUITY OF TONE

Tone is to a story what atmosphere is to a room. The crisp feel of a modernist decor will lose its power if you put a ruffled French couch in its midst. Purity is not an ideal; but a mix, be it in your living room or your writing, has to be carefully considered.

Continuity of tone means that if we're writing a naturalistic novel, we don't suddenly and for no reason employ Gothic mannerisms. Conversely, if we write a Gothic tale, we must not switch into a style of modernist restraint in the second chapter. Continuity matters as much to nonfiction—an intimate memoir I read turned academic two-thirds in. The author knew a lot about a certain field, and his scholarship showboating broke the book's intimacy. If you are writing a serious essay on ethics, you may want to resist throwing in one-liners—which does not mean you should avoid demonstrating a sense of humor; just try to make your humorous tone blend in with the rest of your piece.

We've already seen a good example of tonal breakdown in *The Great Gatsby*: the dramatic, elegant narrative screeched to a halt when monotonous biographical information intruded. The book regained its continuity when Fitzgerald handled the biographical material in the same manner as the other material in the book: dramatically and elegantly.

Continuity of tone may not always serve your purpose, though. We may want to consciously break our tone to create a particular effect. In my former student Miranda Train's story "Desert People," for example, a young woman began a straightforward account of travels with her mother. In a Spanish nightclub the mother embarrassed her daughter by propositioning a waiter. Suddenly, for no apparent reason, the scene went from past to present tense. The tense change occurred midsentence:

"The rest of the night was blurry and plays in flashbacks inside a club with dark walls." I asked the author why she'd made this awkward switch. Train had moved into the present, she explained, to better convey the immediacy of "the flashbacks." If that was her reasoning, the switch was not awkward so much as inadequate. Changing the tense didn't make the flashbacks immediate, and instead caused confusion. I suggested she rough up the text, break more dramatically in tone to achieve the effect she was after. So Train rewrote the flashbacks in disconcerting sentence fragments that better represented the off-kilter feel of the nightclub and of memory. She created two voices: one for day's clarity, another for night's debauchery seen through memory's scrim.

Continuity of tone generally holds a text together and helps it move forward. Sometimes, though, the tone of a work needs to be jumpy. When you edit, ask yourself if your tone fulfills your intention. Editing is not about smoothing out your text at all costs. It is all and only about what works for the project at hand.

Every writer needs to take responsibility for the large strokes of writing. Fitzgerald's editing teaches us the perimeters of a macro-edit. Like him, we need to actively question the clarity and palpability of characters; whether the narrative stalls; whether our structure could be employed to illuminate a theme; if a leitmotiv could be added, or the one in use enhanced; and if there are unwanted tonal breaks. If you are good with details but black out when you step back from your manuscript to see its general shape and conceptual thrust, keep the following list above your desk.

MACRO-EDIT
DIAGNOSTIC CHECKLIST

1. **Intention:** Intention is the overarching aim of a work that guides both writer and reader. Ask yourself when you edit: What is it I want? What am I trying to do here? Where am I going with this?

2. **Character (Palpability, Credibility, Motive):** Make the motives of your main characters clear. Ask of your protagonist: What does she want? If you don't know, develop the character more until you (and the reader) do.

3. **Structure (Rhythm, Tension):** Structure can give your story a beautiful form; more pragmatically, it holds your work together and saves it from collapse.

   Ask yourself when you read your draft: Does the drama feel undramatic? You may need to lengthen or shorten the path to it. A crisis or climax that culminates too early lacks tension, feels schematic and false. Too long a lead-up can kill the reader's interest.

   You may also need to reorder the scenes. Tell a lot up front, you may ruin the story's mystery and the reader's pleasure in discovery; tell too little, the reader may not care about the people in your story enough to want to find out what happens to them.

   Structural diagrams may or may not help you understand the long-term rhythm of your work. Do not obsess over making the perfect starburst or planetary system of narrative elements. Mere doodling or a simple timeline and chapter layout may work as well or better. At their best, diagrams reveal the underpinnings of your project and help modulate your work. At their worst, they distract from the more crucial work of writing and editing prose.

4. **Foreshadowing:** Make whatever you write a page-turner. Insert discreet signals to press the reader's subconscious toward revelation and/or to deepen a theme.

5. **Theme (Leitmotiv):** When you edit, you may want to search out thematic symbols and gingerly sew them into a coherent, barely visible pattern. Laid in with a light touch, leitmotiv can act like a refrain that keeps bringing the reader back to your central theme. The edit is a good place to finesse a leitmotiv, to place it more purposefully and with apt proportions. You may choose a leitmotiv early on, or discover one embedded in your draft when you edit.

6. **Continuity of Tone:** When you read your draft, ask yourself: Are the tone, atmosphere, and characters coherent? Don't let a British accent slur into Brooklynese, for example. Don't let a poetic, ominous atmosphere suddenly and for no good reason turn pedestrian and bright. If your work calls for discontinuity, let the reader know it isn't an accident.

PRACTICE: THE NOTEBOOK (NARRATIVE ELEMENTS)

Keep notebooks on the narrative elements that challenge you. To help with understanding structure, for example, force yourself to find the structure, at least somewhat, of the next book you read, and mark down your findings. The same process may apply to character motive, leitmotiv, and intention. As you edit, check your notebooks for ideas. Use them to ignite your imagination and clarify the mechanisms in your own work.

A Great Luxury
Tracy Kidder

There're so many steps involved in editing and some of them come simultaneously, but if you break them down, first you've got to know that there is something wrong. Forget why or what or anything. Just knowing, "this isn't working" is really important. And then the question is "what's wrong" and "why is it wrong?" And that's not always easy to say, and anyway it doesn't make sense to spend too much time trying to figure that out. If it's wrong it's wrong and what you really want to try to figure out is how to make it right. My usual approach is to rewrite it. And I don't mind that, I like doing that.

I remember trying to tell students, "Look, rewriting is a wonderful thing. It's the only department in life where you get to say something and then take it back and figure out how to say it better before anyone has to see it." And what a great luxury it is. I love rewriting. The kind of rewriting that I generally do is I start over again. Some stuff from the previous draft survives, but I try to find a fresh way to go at something that isn't working.

One of my gripes about the computer is that it encourages a kind of editing that I don't think is very useful. That is, you can move stuff around endlessly. I did a little editing for the late lamented New England Monthly. *Some writer was writing a piece that we really needed and all he kept doing was taking the same bankrupt paragraphs and moving them around.*

~

I went to Andover [prep school] and it was a very rigorous education. You didn't take a test that didn't have essay questions on it. I remember it was really hard trying to learn how to write. And there was an awful lot of rewriting. I learned to rewrite there. I'm grateful for that. I had an English teacher there for a couple of years who made you write an essay topic sentence. By the time you were a senior this seemed absurd. But I don't think it was such a bad idea. It was about figuring out what it is you're really trying to say. I like George Orwell's idea of writing being like a pane of glass.

But the self-critical faculty threatened to become an overdeveloped muscle. When I got to the University of Iowa Writer's Workshop, I was in the class of an awfully fast crowd. I went there thinking I was god's gift to the American novel and discovered that there were dozens who had exactly the same idea. And many of them had a better reason for thinking that than I did. Surrounded by these people, I went silent. I didn't write too much because I was afraid to. I got kind of frozen. There was a much higher standard than I'd been acquainted with. I think it was only there in Iowa that people really got cruel. And I was pretty cruel myself in those workshops, I'm sorry to say.

⌒

My first introduction to someone who was worth listening to as an editor, a real editor, was my friend Stu Dybek, who of all the writers I know comes closest to being objective about any piece of writing, including one that he has created. I never had the impression from him when he was saying, "this is terrible," that he was saying, "you're a terrible writer." It's like that difference that they so often preach but so rarely practice in elementary school teaching, where you attack the behavior of the child and not the child.

A book can be really tender shoots at first. And if you have the wrong kind of editing at that point it can kill it. Kill something that's potentially very good. It's tremendously important to figure out who that other set of eyes ought to be. Because there are people who may actually be envious of you. For instance, that's one thing that they could be. And even though they're really good people and they mean well, their criticism may in fact be in a subconsciously calculated way quite destructive.

I have worked with Dick Todd as my editor for over thirty years. It's very hard for me to sort out what I do with Dick's help and what I do on my own. What happens is, I propose and Dick disposes. There are things that he looks at very closely—proportion: how much of one thing and how much of another. Within the scene or just how many scenes of a certain type. The business of proportion is tremendously important to him. He once said to me, "the whole art of this is making some things big and other things little."

I write as fast as I can so as to prevent remorse for having written badly. And then I rewrite a lot. And poor Todd pretty much sees every draft. I'll show pieces of a first draft to him even, for encouragement. He'll always say great, it's fine, keep going. And then when the whole first draft is done, you'll wonder what it was that he thought was fine.

Then we talk about it and we start over. Usually there's some big problem looming. With The Soul of a New Machine, *I had extremely rich material, it seemed rich to me anyway, and it was about finding those scenes that are literogenic—the scene that could stand for forty others like it.*

With Mountains Beyond Mountains, *mostly there were problems of length and of material that I was just determined to get in. But around the fifth or sixth draft, when it was starting to take some shape and get down to a manageable size, Dick said there was a "problem of goodness." The problem was, how do you write about a guy like Paul Farmer [an infectious-disease doctor who travels the world to heal people with the most needs and the least resources]? How do you make what you believe is true believable to your reader?*

It seemed to me that the first person was absolutely necessary for that. Like a witness saying, "Look, I promise you this is true." I needed some agent to acknowledge the kind of psychological discomfort that anybody a lot less virtuous than this guy is bound to feel in the presence of someone like him, someone so passionate about a cause, someone so self-sacrificing and so gifted. I wanted this narrator to be able to say, in effect, to the reader, "Look I know this guy is beginning to make you feel uneasy, he's making me feel uneasy, too, at this point. And here's what I think about my uneasiness and its causes." And if I did it right, then it would take this "problem of goodness" away and allow the reader to see Farmer as I had finally come to see him and make him as palatable as he ultimately was to me. It was at a kind of late draft that I addressed this, which is when this whole process becomes for me a great deal of fun.

One of the biggest struggles for a young writer, or the biggest struggle for me, was not falling in love with the things that I had written. And I did begin to notice a pattern at some point: the things that I felt were best were the things that really had to be cut. Perhaps there was a psychological mechanism at work, where I was most protective of the things that I knew were most vulnerable or of the things that I had worked hardest on.

The problem is that the pattern's not always right. Sometimes you just found a really nifty way to do something. And there have been times when I have thrown those things away and had to rediscover them later. Sometimes they're good. That's the problem. You can't really be sure. But I think that at a certain point you do get over thinking that anything in a piece of your own writing is precious. It's important to.

III

THE DETAILS: MICRO-EDITING

I had a need to concentrate on each sound,
so that every blade of grass would be
as important as a flower.

Arvo Pärt

In 1959, before he talked about writing, novelist John O'Hara addressed an audience of New Jersey college students about reading: "I read slowly, because when I read . . . I am intently busy. It sometimes takes me half an hour to read a page, because I read first for the story, such as it may be, and then I go back over the page to see how the author got his effects, if he got them; or why he failed, if he did not get them."

For O'Hara, a discussion on writing best began with one on reading. The art of writing (and therefore editing), he knew, rests solidly on the art of reading. The micro-edit in particular thrives on a writer's ability to "read slowly."

But reading as slowly as O'Hara did in 1959 was easier then than now. The concept of being busy had not reached its apogee, as it has in the twenty-first century. To read slowly today is not just unfashionable but nearly impossible. We are in a permanent hurry, and even a move to the sticks cannot protect us from the multiple occupations we administer as members of a global, web-connected community. The Internet helps us be more efficient. But it also compels us to do more things with more people, and have less time to read, let alone slowly. The micro-edit, more than the macro-, demands an unhurried pace. So, when you get to editing the fine details of your text, find it in your twenty-first-century lives to read at O'Hara's speed, circa 1959.

O'Hara also told the Jersey students to "proceed to write . . . , *watching every word along the way.*" Each word, not simply phrase, after all, means something. Every "it," "at," and "for"—and where it gets situated—is a choice. This may seem obvious, but word choice and placement carry even more weight than you might imagine. Take "Jane walked the dog." Or "Jane and the dog went for a walk." These two sentences mean very different things: in the first, Jane dominates; in the second, the dog is Jane's equal. The two sentences are also different in tone. In the first, the syntax is swift and casual. In the second, the sentence is made up of many small, evenly measured one-syllable bits (as opposed to "Jane and the dog went walking") and is, in its regularity, more formal. These sentences about Jane and her pup, on the surface so basic, are no simple textual matter.

You may ask, how do I cross this minefield of meaning? Fortunately, your voice has a sixth sense that will safely guide you much of the way. But voice easily falls in love with itself and, distracted, fails to notice the mines embedded in the page. Micro-editing protects you against your failed sixth sense.

The micro-edit is the once-over you give your text much more than once. You will likely encounter a greater number of errors than in the macro-edit, but they are often simpler to solve than macro-problems.

Are you a natural macro- or micro-editor? Figure out if your strength is in the large picture or the details. Now take your strength and put it on a high shelf. Concentrate on the kind of editing that isn't easy for you, the kind you may even hate. I was not a natural macro-editor, and, in my youth, skirted the macro-issues of text whenever possible. Eventually, I forced myself to sit still long enough with a piece of writing for the macro-silhouette to reveal itself. I did this again and again until macro-editing, though still challenging, no longer frightened me. Natural-born macro-editors, who see the whole forest but not its parts, also need to sit and stare; they need to learn to read patiently and thoroughly, over and over again, until they see the bugs on the grass.

Fitzgerald was a natural micro-editor. He continually sought out the weak phrasings in his work and strengthened them. His micro-edits are a literary trove, from which we learn that the smallest errors can lead a writer to develop and deepen his material in unexpected ways. *The Great Gatsby*, in early drafts, displayed countless micro-mistakes: overemphasis, cliché, pedestrian language, generic and inauthentic dialogue. Fitzgerald edited his prose until virtually every phrase meant something essential and sounded fresh.

Since Max Perkins mainly addressed *The Great Gatsby*'s conceptual problems, his letters carry little evidence of Fitzgerald's microscopic edits. The evidence shows up, though, when we compare early manuscript drafts to the final one. Since *The Great Gatsby* does not offer before-and-after editing examples for every micro-element listed below, we will occasionally review examples from other authors.

MICRO-VIEW

1. Language
2. Repetition
3. Redundancy
4. Clarity
5. Authenticity: image, dialogue
6. Continuity: visuals, character
7. Show and tell
8. Beginnings, endings, transitions

LANGUAGE

Language reigns over every micro–narrative element. Repetitions, clarity, authenticity, demonstrative action—all involve the careful use of language, but language is something more than just the sum of these parts. Language is, in a word, voice. It determines that transcendent aspect of a writer's work, that unique style that for a painter emerges in the palette and stroke, and for a writer in the lexicon and syntax. Every choice we make, large and small, what we leave out and what we leave in a piece of writing, for instance, defines us, but our words and sentence design may be the most salient signs of our voice. Our true voice—that is, one unalloyed by mimicry or pretension—is what gives our writing its dignity.

Rooted in habit, however, language can be cumbersome to maneuver. Your individual linguistic style/voice has formed over the course of your life. For years we string particular words together in a particular order, until we end up mimicking ourselves. Our writing is at service to a script ingrained in us since our early youth. The seminal designer Kaj Franck used to tell his students, "Paint a pretty picture. Pick your own subject. But you can't use any of your favourite colours." One woman wondered why she had to give up lemon yellow—she couldn't paint without it, she said. Franck's aim, an acolyte explained, was to "liberate students from acquired mannerisms or conventional aesthetics, anything that blocks original expression." With a similar motive, writers may need to edit out favorite riffs to force themselves to really *write*—not merely record the verbal mannerisms stored in the brain.

Our use of language is profoundly personal; still, there exist among us common mistakes. The following four tenets may help you avoid them.

Keep language fresh

Clichés can be rampant in early drafts. "All writing," according to Martin Amis, "is a campaign against cliché. Not just clichés of the pen but clichés of the mind and clichés of the heart. When I dispraise, I am usually quoting clichés. When I praise, I am usually quoting the opposed qualities of freshness, energy, and reverberation of voice."

Listen:

> It was no good anymore. It was no use pretending. We couldn't make it together. She and I had a breakdown in communication. We just couldn't go on. I wanted out. I was going nuts about my future. She could break loose and start over. No matter how much I wanted to live on the edge, I had to buckle down and come up with the goods for my boss. I've been broken up about it for months.

Any one of these sentences, let alone their aggregate, deserves "dispraise" because you've heard them before, perhaps twenty thousand times. Reread your text for clichés. Ask yourself if your language is your own, or if you bought it from a verbal superstore.

One last, more positive note on clichés. Deadening clichés can be refreshed by an author's ingenuity. Take the scene at the Plaza Hotel, where Gatsby tells Tom, " 'No, [Daisy and I] couldn't meet. But both of us loved each other all that time, old sport, and you didn't know. I used to laugh sometimes'—but there was no laughter in his eyes—'to think that you didn't know.' " The phrase "there was no laughter in his eyes" is a cliché, but Fitzgerald's odd placement of it—as an unlikely break in the dialogue—renews it. He restores an element of surprise to the words by putting them in a surprising place.

Keep language precise and concise

Avoid rhetoric that sounds lofty, says little, and obscures your meaning. Fitzgerald wrote, for example, "I was thirty. Beside that realization their importunities were dim and far away. Before me stretched the portentous menacing road of a new decade." The author edited out the second sentence; he must have seen that "realization" and "importunities" were blousy generalities that didn't add important meaning, and distracted the reader from the real point: Nick's fear of aging. Once that second sentence is gone, the paragraph is cleaner: "I was thirty. Before me stretched the portentous, menacing road of a new decade." We move fluidly through Fitzgerald's edited prose, undetained by filler.

Most detrimental to precision and concision are adverbs and adjectives. Terms like "really," "very," beautiful," "wonderfully," "truly," "amazing," "awful" rarely help your prose: "It was really fun; I'm very angry she came; she used to be a very beautiful person. It's truly amazing how she has changed. We were wonderfully happy." Modifiers are often overused, vague, or superfluous, or all three. They mollify a sentence instead of strengthen it. As you edit, try removing adverbs and adjectives. Much of the time sentences will sound more vigorous without them. On occasion, you will find an adjective or adverb brings vital emphasis or meaning to a sentence. (Take the one I just wrote. In it, the adjective "vital" sharpened its meaning.) A modifier proves its worth when, in its absence, a sentence slackens. Then, of course, keep it.

The same rule of necessity goes for tiny words that clog sentences.

She promised **that** she would stop me. } She promised she would stop me.

This is a fine mess **that** you are in. } This is a fine mess you are in.

In spite of the fact that I cook, I don't like to eat. } Though I cook, I don't like to eat.

I pulled the plug **in order to** see if he'd yell. } I pulled the plug to see if he'd yell.

I would argue that wordy sentences do not work. } Wordy sentences do not work.

In the last instance, notice how the writer inadvertently reveals his self-doubt. By using the phrase "I would argue that," he mitigates his idea and the reader senses the author's uncertainty. Commit to your ideas; be certain enough to write them without wordy precautions, announcements, or apologies. "I would argue that" is meaningless rhetoric, since you inherently argue your ideas by writing them down. The reader, by virtue of reading, wants those ideas, and not peripheral verbiage.

Many writing mishaps could be avoided if a writer thought harder about the notion of necessity—in other words, about language that is, or isn't, necessary. I think back to an exercise I did in theater school. The actors were told to create a dramatic scene and then act it out, but there was a catch: we were forbidden to use words. We did the scene in silence for a week. In the second week, we were asked to act out the same scene and add words. After having worked in silence for so long, we had learned to express ourselves with our body, our will, our intention. When, at last, we were free to use words, we hardly needed them. We chose to say only what we could not express in any other manner.

This exercise in verbal economy might well be applied to editing text. We might edit away much of our prose and see how our scene plays spare. With potential excesses removed, we can compare before and after versions to see which works better. Sometimes it's a toss-up. Both versions may sound good. That's when it's useful to recall the actors who did their scene in silence and ask: Is this word, phrase, paragraph *necessary*?

In an early draft of *Gatsby*, for instance, Fitzgerald wrote three unnecessary words into the sentence "His first instinct made him step hard on the accelerator." After editing, it read, "Instinct made him step on the accelerator." Pluck three simple words and you can expose the muscle of a sentence.

(Dialogue, however, comes to life from normal speech—superfluity, stutters, and all. To edit dialogue is to focus on authenticity before concision. The rule of necessity still applies, but it may be necessary, in order to be genuine, to include linguistic excess or errance.)

Whether minimalist or maximalist, it is essential to know when you are indulging a word or phrase you love for the sake of it. Let go of your lemon yellow. "Let go," as Faulkner said, "of your darlings."

Keep language active and erect

Certain words have good posture, others slump. Present participles, or what I call the "ing" words, tend to slump.

> I was shaking my head, thinking about how stupid I'd been } I shook my head and thought about how stupid I'd been.
>
> He was drinking seltzer, shying away from the beer } He drank seltzer and shied away from the beer.
>
> You were singing in the rain, so I was listening } You were singing in the rain, so I listened.
>
> We were hiding your present as you were opening the door } We were hiding your present as you opened the door.
>
> They are arriving tonight } They arrive tonight.

The verb "to be" is a lazy verb that uses present participles to modify itself. The combination thickens sentences unnecessarily. In large doses, "to be" reveals an author's unwillingness or inability to energize his writing with livelier verbs, and "ing" words compound the problem. Of the two sentences, "We are dancing today at six" or "we dance today at six," which sounds stronger?

Of course there are times when the present participle is our only choice—because an action is drawn out or repeated in the present tense, or for rhythm. "You sang in the rain, so I listened" may be better with a present participle left in: "You were singing in the rain, so I listened." The perfect past tense, "sang," implies an action that began and ended quickly, whereas the song probably went on for a while. I also prefer the asymmetrical sentence rhythm here of one "ing" left in. But sentences often do better with no present participle at all: "She kicked me as I slept." "They arrive tonight." With their "ing"s and "to be"s gone, verbs spring upright.

Another common "ing" construction creates a linguistic standstill: "He drank until dawn, becoming giddy with the girls." Or "They tore off the wrappers, their hunger distracting them from the sound of the key in the door." In the first clause, the action moves forward, only to get pulled back in the second by the present participle. In other words, the "ing" clause blunts the sentence's initial thrust by extending the action. Try, "He drank until dawn and became giddy with the girls." Or "As they tore off the wrappers, their hunger distracted them from the sound of the key in the door." Here, one action follows another, and the reader gets caught up in the momentum. The "standstill" construction can work. But it may be less elegant than others. Most troubling, many writers use it at every turn, and whatever finesse they had evaporates with the repetition of that one construct.

Although the present participle, especially as a modifier, can be useful, it is habit-forming. Editing is the only solution. Develop your editor's eye to see where your words slouch.

Keep language real

Avoid overwriting or pretention. Have you succumbed to a self-conscious choice of word or syntax? Does your work, or any part of it, feel artificial, effortful, irritating?

Like this: "We went zooming across the iridescent fields, navigating amongst the bellowing bonfires until the nature of fire and light had entered us and unbeknownst to our impertinent parents who had never appreciated the filial affection and respect we had bestowed upon their anachronistic Machiavellian selves, we bloomed and alighted upon a new era." If we let the air out, we might get something like this: "We zoomed across the fields and made our way between bonfires that made the earth into the sun; we absorbed the light, as our changeless parents slept unknowing, and aimed it at a new era." The second version still has a pulse and mystical feel, but also a discipline that the first lacked. The first is rife with clichés and phrases overly formal—unless spoken by someone in a past century ("we bloomed," "alighted upon," "unbeknownst," "amongst," "bestowed upon"), and vague (what exactly is "the nature of fire and light"? and how could it "enter us"?). The mixed imagery sounds sloppy too: "We went zooming" and "we bloomed." Are we a car or a flower? The sentence contains too many adjectives: iridescent, bellowing, impertinent, filial, anachronistic, Machiavellian. And the repetition of "ing"s at the start: "We went zooming . . . , navigating amongst" is cumbrous compared to "We zoomed . . . and made our way." I rewrote that overblown line with two goals: to keep its energy and distill its meaning. In the first sentence, the metaphor of light is incoherent. It was necessary to make a light that did not float around as a self-important, pretty idea, but had specific meaning. The revised light has become precise and consistent.

A writer's language largely forms a reader's experience. A sexy, shocking story told in uninspired prose will bore. Content is not worth much until a writer funnels it through a voice that has been clarified and deepened through editing.

REPETITION

Repetitions of words or expressions are only acceptable when the author designs them for a reason. While Fitzgerald purposely repeated "old sport" until it became a leitmotiv, his repetition of "self-controll" [*sic*] in the following passage was an accident. In an early draft of *Gatsby*, the confrontation scene read:

"He isn't causing any row," whispered Daisy tensely, "You're causing a row. Please have a little **self-controll**."

"**Self-controll!**" repeated Tom incredulously, "**Self-controll.!**"

"That's it," said Daisy brightly . . .

. . . For a moment I thought she was going to get him away but unfortunately Gatsby who hadn't said a word looked up at Daisy suddenly with adoring eyes.

"**Self-controll**," repeated Tom sardonically, "I suppose the latest thing is to sit back and let Mr. Nobody from nowhere make love to your wife. . . . "

In the final version, the author scrapped two of his four "self-control"s (and also corrected his spelling):

"He isn't causing a row." Daisy looked desperately from one to the other.

"You're causing a row. Please have a little **self-control**."

"**Self-control!**" repeated Tom incredulously. "I suppose the latest thing is to sit back and let Mr. Nobody from Nowhere make love to your wife."

Fitzgerald condensed the scene and more carefully measured his repetition, which made this passage more pointed and authoritative.

A less pronounced but still egregious repetition showed up when Gatsby confided his past to Nick: "The part of his life he told me about **began when** he was sixteen, **when** the popular songs of those days **began** to assume for him a melancholy and romantic beauty." This sentence may seem alright as it is, but I dare any reader to argue its elegance. Fitzgerald would delete it altogether.

If, when you are editing, you find your words have hardened into the wrong shape, and you cannot make them budge, try a rearranging game: see how many different ways you can say the same thing. You could try, "He told me about the part of his life that began when he was sixteen . . . " or "He told me when he was sixteen the popular songs of those days . . . " or "He told me about his life at sixteen, when the popular songs of those days . . . " or "The popular songs of those days, he told me, began to assume for him a melancholy and romantic beauty when he was sixteen." You may well nix them all, but the effort will have jiggled your brain, and very soon you will reinvent the passage to your satisfaction. Fitzgerald rewrote it like this: "It was this night that he told me the strange story of his youth with Dan Cody—told it to me because 'Jay Gatsby' had broken up like glass against Tom's hard malice, and the long secret extravaganza was played out."

Fitzgerald would not be satisfied to simply polish the given parts of his prose; he would raise the entire level of a sentence. The startling image of an exposed and shattered Gatsby, of a man made of glass breaking up against another man's hard stone, of the failure of a "long secret extravaganza," added immeasurable power to a previously dull passage.

Simple repetition can, like cliché, work in a writer's favor. "There is no **confusion** like the **confusion** of a simple mind," says Nick, for example, in reference to Tom (chapter seven). Soon after, Nick repeats another significant word in close proximity to its first utterance: "I was **thirty**." And four sentences later: "**Thirty**—the promise of . . . " This is stylish, rhetorical repetition that creates emphasis, as well as a musical beat.

Words are not the only issue. Take care not to indiscriminately repeat a turn of phrase. Avoid, that is, overusing one particular sentence structure, such as, for example, a clause, then a colon, then a list. Single out the structure you unwittingly repeat, enter it in a notebook marked "patterns to break," and make it the only thing you look for on one or two read-throughs. Hunt down your habit, and train your mind to flinch at it.

REDUNDANCY

This is the repetition of an idea, as opposed to a word or phrasing. Good readers don't need to be told something again and again, if it is suggested or told clearly in the first place. Do not confuse redundancy with leitmotiv. While leitmotiv repeats a theme undercover, as it were, disguised as a word or image, redundancy brazenly repeats an idea on the surface of the text.

There are three types of redundant writers. One lacks inspiration, so writes something he has already written, only in different words. His redundancy is filler. The second type suffers from misguided generosity. This writer has found three fabulous ways to say something, and cannot deny any of them to the world. He uses all he's got instead of making a choice. Readers, though, cannot absorb too many riches at once, when they all convey nearly the same meaning.

The third redundant writer suffers from distraction, brought on by fatigue or intense concentration. Distracted, the writer repeats himself in different words and never notices. Here, in an early draft of *Gatsby*, is one subtle example of what I would guess to be the last type:

> He might have despised himself, for he had certainly [taken] her under false pretenses. I don't mean **he had claimed to be young Gatsby son of a mythical millionaire,** old Gatsby, but he had deliberately given Daisy a sense of security about him; he let her believe that he was a person from much the same stratum as herself and that in case of any emergency he was able to take care of her. As a matter of fact he had no such facilities—**he had no comfortable family standing behind him** . . .

In the early draft, an idea is simply repeated, not grown: Gatsby is not the son of a rich man both at the start of the paragraph ("[not the] son of a mythical millionaire, old Gatsby"), and again at the end of it ("he had no comfortable family standing behind him"). That Gatsby is not heir to a fortune is given twice in different words. In the final version, Fitzgerald wrote:

> He might have despised himself, for he had certainly taken her under false pretenses. I don't mean that **he had traded on his phantom millions**, but he had deliberately given Daisy a sense of security; he let her believe that he was a person from much the same stratum as herself—that

he was fully able to take care of her. As a matter of fact, he had no such facilities—**he had no comfortable family standing behind him** . . .

Here, Fitzgerald's description of Gatsby evolves with each sentence, from general to precise. First, we learn Gatsby is false: "he had . . . taken her under false pretenses"; then, we learn he is falsely rich: he has "phantom millions"; but then, in the next clause, the falsehood is made even more precise: it is not money in the simple sense, but the status and security it buys that Gatsby falsely traded on: "he let her believe that he was . . . from much the same stratum as herself" and could, under any circumstance, "take care of her." At this point, the passage culminates in a fresh, sharp point about money: "he had no comfortable family standing behind him." Gatsby has no *old* money, the loftiest kind. Instead of, as in the early draft, telling us this at the start of the paragraph only to repeat it at the end, the author steadily leads us up to it. By making us discover something after a series of incremental steps, he creates a far more compelling passage.

Just as calculated repetition can be stylish, so can calculated redundancy. A writer may wish to subvert the traditional authority of fiction or nonfiction by offering multiple versions of one idea. Think of Kurosawa's *Rashomon*, the film in which characters give their very different accounts of the same crime. Similarly, Bradford Morrow, in his short story "Lush," repeats one incident—a car accident—as it is viewed differently by three different characters: the woman who dies in the crash, the woman who doesn't, and the widowed man who was not at the scene. Morrow's redundancy exposes the impossibility of a writer telling something in a truly accurate light. Redundancy and repetition shape the opening of Luc Sante's memoir *The Factory of Facts*, where the author repeats his family history nine times, with significant if small variations. Sante makes history redundant and therefore questionable. What *really* happened? Sante seems to ask. Which is the best way to tell it? Is the best way to tell it more important than what really happened?

Redundancy can be a useful subversive device. Your edit is the time to make sure you have chosen your crime, however, not simply discovered it by accident.

CLARITY

Muddled meaning is a plague among inexperienced writers, and well within reach of some veterans. Somerset Maugham wrote in *The Summing Up*: "[A cause] of obscurity is that the writer is himself not quite sure of his meaning. He has a vague impression of what he wants to say, but has not . . . exactly formulated it in his mind, and it is natural enough that he should not find a precise expression for a confused idea." If you cannot say clearly what you mean, you are not clear about your meaning. Clear thinking makes for clear writing.

A prep school headmaster once told me that for many teachers, writing student evaluations did not come easy. "For people who have trouble writing," he said, "the problem is ontological." If a person is not clear about himself, how can he be clear about his subject? The headmaster's reasoning was surely too pat, but he was on to something. What we are informs what we mean. If we are in a state of confusion, so will be what we write. Some teachers, for example, might want to please a parent, take down an irreverent child, come off more or less imperious or intellectual than usual. Confused motives easily lead to confused—unfocused or convoluted—prose. To be clear, we must be natural. Anyone with a pen risks writing to an ideal instead of naturally. Before you can write clearly, then, you must be clear about who you are and what you are after in your work. Much of the time, we aren't clear about these things until we edit. Editing is the place where we sweep away the confusions we felt as we wrote. We force ourselves to narrow down our possibilities, to declare our mission, know clearly what we do and don't want to say and sound like.

A good way to become clear, after writing a dense, meandering draft of an essay, story, or chapter, is to ask yourself: What are the three main points I want to communicate? Just three, no more. Reread your draft with those points in mind, and you'll suddenly see the extraneous matter that needs cutting. (This method works best with nonfiction.) We often write two, three, or four times the ideas that our piece can effectively hold. Revel in the chance to edit out most ideas, until the essential ones can emerge and develop.

After you've settled on what's essential to keep, you need to check, when you edit, the order of things. I often find, for instance, that the first sentence to my paragraph is buried in the middle of it, and I need to move it to the top. By placing my summary thought at the start of a paragraph, I'm helping my reader follow, helping my point come up clear instead of being an afterthought. Leaving my paragraph written exactly as it came to me can sometimes work; but other times, it's confusing. I first wrote this paragraph, for example, for the upcoming section on continuity:

Discontinuity shows up not just in details, but in voice. Daisy's authenticity, for example, broke down with the discontinuity of her voice in the exchange about the Dashiels. Continuity of voice and authenticity of character often overlap. Without the former it is impossible to have the latter.

I edited it into this:

> Continuity of voice and authenticity of character often overlap. The authenticity of Daisy's character broke down, for instance, with the discontinuity of her voice in the exchange about the Dashiels.

Once the clear idea surfaced, it wasn't hard to sweep away the excess around it.

Fitzgerald's first forays onto the page were sometimes ambiguous. It is worth parsing for one last time a passage we've already looked at from different angles. There is no better example of how to give muddled prose clarity than the scene where Nick and Jordan listen to Gatsby, Daisy, and Tom bicker in the Plaza Hotel. In an early draft, Nick says,

> I was thirty. Beside that realization their importunities were dim and far away. Before me stretched the portentous menacing road of a new decade.

A few paragraphs later, he rides home with Jordan in a taxi, and adds:

> I was thirty—a decade of loneliness opened up suddenly before me and what had hovered between us was said at last in the pressure of a hand.

Fitzgerald is trying to conjure Nick up, reveal his deepest concerns, but Nick remains hazy. His thoughts are opaque; a threat looms, but he does not say what it is. When he says "what had hovered between us was said at last in the pressure of a hand," he is suggesting there's something serious between him and Jordan, but what exactly is it? Whatever's hovering between them is held off at a distance. By removing the words "realization," "importunities," and "portentous," the writing is instantly more precise. And precision and clarity go hand in hand. Fitzgerald deleted the second sentence of the paragraph to focus on one main point: "Before me stretched the portentous menacing road of a new decade."

A few paragraphs later, Nick is in the taxi as before, but this time he picks up the dangling thread—the undefined threat—and sews it in:

> Thirty—**the promise of a decade of loneliness, a thinning list of single men to know, a thinning brief case of enthusiasm, thinning hair.** But there was **Jordan** beside me, who, **unlike Daisy, was too wise ever to carry well-forgotten dreams from age to age.** As we passed over the dark bridge her wan face fell lazily against my coat's shoulder and **the formidable stroke of thirty died away with the reassuring pressure of her hand.**

Fitzgerald took a couple of wordy, imprecise sentences and transformed them into a crisp exposé of a single idea: the loss of youth. The danger of turning thirty is at last defined. The disillusionment that comes with age underscores the character descriptions, instead of being a coarse intellectual aside. And the final sentence, a detached commentary on a detached relationship, becomes, through editing, a commitment to human tenderness, however flawed. By changing "a hand" to "her hand," Fitzgerald creates a truer intimacy and offers the poignant conclusion that human affection alone can compensate for the indignities of growing old.

Clarity, then, comes from the razing of superfluity, but also from the development of an idea. Knowing where to expand your text is as important as knowing where to shrink it.

A common obstacle to clarity is the fear of looking stupid. Many of my students complain their readers miss their point. These writers want to be understood, yet not too understood. They want to be subtle. But subtlety can lead us astray. As commonly preached in every beginner's writing class and worth repeating: do not assume the reader knows what you know. Also, don't forget process: to end up subtle you may first need to place your heart (or brain) on your sleeve, then selectively pull it off bit by bit, until only some tiny potent piece is left there. It is very hard to see the right tiny piece to leave until you see the whole thing spread out in front of you.

Writers who like to distinguish between "high" and "low" art, and put themselves safely on the mount, are most likely to suffer from being overly subtle. These writers believe "high" means to be restrained or coy and "low" means saying it plain and straight. But concepts of high and low only corner a writer. Restraint is elegant and noble, but plain and straight can be too. One of America's most erudite, poetic essayists, Eliot Weinberger, for instance, wrote an essay of over ten thousand words where nearly every short paragraph begins with the words "I heard," after which the writer baldly states the facts:

I heard the vice president say: "By any standard of even the most dazzling charges in military history, the Germans in the Ardennes in the spring of 1940 or Patton's romp in July of 1944, the present race to Baghdad is unprecedented in its speed and daring and in the lightness of casualties."

I heard Colonel David Hackworth say: "Hey diddle diddle, it's straight up the middle!"

I heard the Pentagon spokesman say that 95 percent of the Iraqi casualties were "military-age males."

I heard an official from the Red Crescent say: "On one stretch of highway alone, there were more than fifty civilian cars, each with four or five people incinerated inside, that sat in the sun for ten or fifteen days before they were buried nearby by volunteers. That is what there will be for their relatives to come and find. War is bad, but its remnants are worse."

The power of Weinberger's "What I Heard About Iraq" lies in the carefully structured accumulation of countless hideous and often shocking revelations. Weinberger refuses lyricism and coyness—typically associated with sophisticated writing—to impress you instead with what's true. In twenty-first-century America, where the obvious truth goes ignored, stating it simply and unequivocally is not so obvious. It is the essay's concept, structure, and rhythm that are subtle, not its language—largely ungilded reportage. Weinberger's radical simplicity instructs us to toss out our preset ideas of what it means to be and write smart. His tactics result in clarity at its most elegant. (The essay also provides a fine example of stylish repetition.)

The fear of looking stupid leads to another form of muddle:

the sentence-stuffed-like-a-turkey syndrome. Many writers stuff five ideas into one sentence because they think the more the smarter. One simple idea, they believe, will sound inadequate, and worse, banal. But when you put too many ideas into one sentence, each loses its distinction. A battle for attention ensues, where each idea kills off the other and none win. Do not be afraid of being spare. Did Beckett write many long, compacted sentences? Try this one about Jordan in *The Great Gatsby*: "She was incurably dishonest." Four words in one clause; no commas, colons, semicolons, or dashes. A sentence so curt, yet it conveys everything we ever need to know about Jordan. Also, the two words "incurably dishonest" call out the very theme of the book: the incurable dishonesty of American life, the sham of America's capitalistic dream that destroys any honest love and lover in its path. Fitzgerald's sentence is simple but hardly bland. If you've written a bird's nest, then, untangle your ideas. Separate them into a few sentences. One small sentence, written well, can tell more than an expansive one that's gangly.

If long, convoluted sentences are your natural bent, though, I am not here to sway you in a different direction. I'm here to remind maximalists to think about being clear as well as complex. When you edit, check to see that you're using the long, curvaceous sentence to say something, not as a catchall for the numerous ideas you've been unable to tease out and trim. In works by writers such as Dave Hickey, Virginia Woolf, and Henry James, convoluted phrasing, in essays or fiction, succeed at conveying meaning as clear as glass. In *The Spoils of Poynton*, James writes, "Knowing the church to be near, she prepared in her room for the little rural walk, and on her way down again, passing through corridors and observing imbecilities of decoration, the aesthetic misery of the big commodious house, she felt a return of the tide of last night's irritation, a renewal of everything she could secretly suffer from ugliness and stupidity." This sentence is the alter ego to Fitzgerald's four-word wonder. Both work. Although James writes long, he grows each idea from the one that precedes it. The reader does not feel assaulted by the quantity of ideas, but drawn into the logical, linear sweep of them. Complication in and of itself does not preclude clarity. But baroque prose demands tremendous rigor from the writer. If you stuff a sentence, you must know how to do so with complementary ingredients—ideas that do not compete but play off one another. Above all, as you edit, concentrate on determining when enough is enough.

Neville Wakefield likes to go overboard in his writing, then use editing to tuck in the flaps of his piece. His sentence about Daido Moriyama's New York City photographs is a perfect example:

Their record is less the monuments that loom all around, than the transient ephemeral social architecture that fills the spaces in between—the pungent odors that hold the back seat of the cab after its occupant is long gone: the rodent citadels of garbage that pour onto the unclaimed sidewalk; the product-filled vitrines whose advertisements to consume stand between over lit bodega interiors and the flow of opportunism and dereliction on the other side.

As Wakefield's editor, my challenge was to respect his lyrical complexity even as I helped him comb out and clarify his meanings; then, sometimes, give those meanings a shave. I would not turn his long sentences into another writer's short ones—this was

Neville's piece, not someone else's and least of all mine. Here is how Neville's piece ended up, not much different from the original, just more transparent:

> They record less the monuments that loom all around than the intermittent social architecture that fills the spaces in between—the pungent odors that hold the back seat of the cab after its occupant is long gone; the rodent citadels of garbage that pour onto the unclaimed sidewalk; the product-filled vitrines of overlit bodegas that advertise to the street as they conceal the store within.

Remember to punctuate your languor with rest spots—the reader needs to breathe. You can rhythmically hold on to him by controlling the musical measure of your prose. As you edit, watch out for long-winded areas, where you lose track of and even interest in the content of what may be beautifully turned sentences. You may want to mete out short sentences amid the long, like sorbet served between the courses of a rich meal.

As editors, we must take care not to dumb down a text as we refine it. Mystery and poetic ambiguities enrich a work. Authority is key. Even avant-gardists who wish to debunk narrative authority must fuel their own writing with it.

When you edit, determine what is mystery and what is muddle; the first to be respected and left alone, the second to be respected and cleaned up. Any kind of sentence may work: long or short, loopdelooped or gimleted, so long as it reflects the author's clarity of mind—a clarity that often comes as you edit, and not before.

AUTHENTICITY: IMAGE, DIALOGUE

Writing that is authentic is credible, and without credibility your reader will abandon you in a blink. The imagery and dialogue of your piece, fictional or not, must be true, for instance, to the time period, social atmosphere, and economic class of your characters.

Most of all, the people in your writing need to feel authentic. John O'Hara said, "The basic, indispensable attribute of a novelist is the understanding of character and the ability to create characters." The same could be said of the short story writer, memoirist, and biographer. Unless you are writing for artificial effect, use imagery details and dialogue to help make your characters lifelike.

"Tell me what you eat," eighteenth-century philosopher-cum-gastronomist Brillat-Savarin said, "and I will tell you who you are." More commonly put, we are what we eat. In writing, we are what we eat, drink, wear; where we sleep, sit, dine, etc. Details give your work texture, depth, and credibility. When you edit, ask yourself: Would this character really drive an SUV? Eat crème fraîche? Sit in an Eames chair, wear pearls, use a fancy pen, sleep on a futon, drink cheap Scotch?

Authentic details can perform nice feats of indirection. Say you write an account of the days you spent living with a group of anti-American revolutionaries in Pakistan. You recall that at a meeting cigarettes were passed around. Were they local bidis or an expensive American brand? American cigarettes in the hands of anti-American fanatics present a fascinating contradiction. Did the leader wear a Rolex? The details indirectly make the point, and the reader has more fun interpreting them than being told what to think. The reader's thoughts will run deeper if he assembles them for himself. Finally, it is better to let details speak, than to judge or explain your characters with your intellect. You can do no better than to authentically present them.

O'Hara, still lecturing to those college students, described an intriguing short story he once wrote

> in which no human being appeared. I described in detail, in significant detail, the contents of a hotel room. . . . When you finish reading the story you know that the man who had been occupying the room had been on the town the night before, that he had quarreled with his girl, and that he had committed suicide by jumping out the window.

Detail is so potent that one could tell a story with nothing but. When you edit, remove the random details. Significant details are the ones that describe more than what is visual. There is Gatsby's hair, for example, which looks like it's clipped every day. Choose the detail that has an echo behind it.

"Detail has to be handled with care," says O'Hara. "For instance when you are describing a man's clothes you must get everything right, especially the wrong thing." He offered this example: A man in the 1940s wears a well-cut, nicely fitting, double-breasted suit; a quiet, striped shirt from a London shirt-maker; and a small-figured necktie. But instead of the customary gold safety pin in his collar, he wears a miniature hunting horn. The hunting horn pin signifies wealth of the sort who likes to fox hunt. But a true gentleman would only wear his horn in the field during a hunt; by wearing it with his expensive suit to town, he flaunts his hunter status. The man doesn't know the unspoken rules of aristocracy. The pin has tipped us off that he is a phony.

Encoded, or as O'Hara calls them, "significant," details abound in *Gatsby*. The pearls Tom buys at the end indicate his continuous infidelity. Daisy already had pearls, we saw her wear them earlier in the book; this new strand must be for someone else. More symbolically, the cuff links of human teeth worn by Gatsby's gangster boss indicate all we ever need to know about the wearer's moral code.

Details may be many or few, but best not to shovel them in wholesale. Your obligation as an editor, for yourself or for another, is to carefully select details that both mean the most and are the most authentic.

Dialogue, like detail, offers the chance to build or destroy a character's credibility. For some writers, authentic dialogue poses the hardest challenge of writing. Yet, it cannot be overlooked, for "nothing," says O'Hara, "could so quickly cast doubt on, and even destroy, an author's characters as bad dialogue. If the people did not talk right, they were not real people. The closer to real talk, the closer to real people."

When you reread your text, ask yourself: Do people really say that? Or have you written dialogue you've seen in cartoons or books, heard in movies? Listen to the people around you; as you edit, try to match the authenticity of what you've heard with what you write. Listen harder to your own characters—as they respond to a given situation, let them talk before you put words in their mouth.

Fitzgerald, in an early draft, wrote dialogue as authentic as a trout that suddenly lays salmon eggs. At the Plaza Hotel, Daisy and Gatsby argue:

"That's it," said Daisy brightly,

"What's more if we're going to the Dashboards tonight we ought to be starting home."

"What Dashboards?"

"I don't know. They're your friends. You ought to—"

"You mean the Dashiels. Austin Dashiel."

"Well, whoever they are. You made the engagement and if you want to keep it we'd be—"

This is stilted, flat filler, but more importantly, inauthentic to Daisy's character. Daisy is flaky and weak, but never stupid. Throughout the novel, she makes witty remarks that counter the dumb-blonde cliché that would easily have defined her in a less able author's hands. It is her surprising wit that makes Daisy so compelling: she is a will-o'-the-wisp with a swift left hook. Listen to her elsewhere in the book: "Open the whiskey, Tom, and I'll make you a mint julep. Then you won't seem so stupid to yourself." Or,

> Daisy: "Open another window."
> Jordan: "There aren't anymore."
> Daisy: "Well, we'd better telephone for an axe."

Or Daisy cries out from Gatsby's car to Tom's,

> "Where are we going?"
> Tom's group: "How about the movies?"
> Daisy: "It's so hot. You go. We'll ride around and meet you after. . . . We'll meet you on some corner. I'll be the man smoking two cigarettes."

The Dashboard joke is beneath the "real" Daisy, who may be silly but not flat-footed. The whole exchange about the Dashiels was incidental in a book where everything means something, and sure enough, Fitzgerald deleted it.

O'Hara denigrates the use of taped conversations as a method to improve one's dialogue because dialogue must do more than record exactly what someone said. It must be massaged into an element that, as he puts it, "creat[es] and maintain[s] character, [advances] a story, and [gives] life to a scene." Sometimes it behooves a writer to write exactly what he hears. Usually, though, he's better off embellishing or cutting back on it, shaping it to suit a scene. In O'Hara's own *Appointment in Samarra*, two young boys are running from the police and one says to the other, "Well, if you go home—they know who you are at the store—so if you go home they'll have the cop, Leffler, he'll wait there for you." The boy's panic is beautifully embodied by his interrupted and incomplete sentences. People, panicked or not, usually speak the way they think, which is often disjointedly. They also punctuate their spoken sentences with "um," "okay," "you know," "basically," "like," "mmm," and "uh." To transcribe these utterances verbatim to the page would waylay the reader. O'Hara knew better than to replicate every "y'know." Some of the worst dialogue attempts authenticity by using "um" and "uh" to signal that a character is speaking naturally. Instead, the reader is alerted that the writer is trying too hard.

The choices we make with dialogue are about rhythm, subject matter, character development, and humor, not just credibility. "L'exactitude," said painter Henri Matisse, "n'est pas la vérité." Truth is not exactitude. We need to edit a character's speech so that it walks the very thin line between artifice and documentary.

CONTINUITY: VISUALS, CHARACTER

Writing demands so very much of us at all times that some one aspect of the process is sure to short-circuit at any given moment. The least profound, but nevertheless annoying, blowouts have to do with continuity.

Continuity is best understood by discussing its opposite. Discontinuity shows up when a black dog on page 4 is brown on page 200. Or a woman tells her husband on page 10 she's going to the doctor on Tuesday afternoon, but on page 120 she refers to Tuesday afternoon's bridge game. It is hard to recall every tiny thing you put down, and keep it right a hundred pages later. In the movie business, a continuity professional will make sure an actress is wearing the same red dress throughout one scene, even if the scene is shot over the course of seven days. But if you are writing on your own, without a publishing contract, you have to be your own continuity professional. If you have a publisher, you could leave it to the copy editor to find your slipups, but this is risky. Some copy editors work with remarkable finesse, some are sloppy. You cannot control which kind you get.

Continuity of voice and authenticity of character often overlap. Let's go back to Daisy. The authenticity of her character broke down with the discontinuity of her voice in the exchange about the Dashiels. In another example of discontinuity, Nick, in an early draft, described Tom's state of mind while they drove to Manhattan:

> In spite of all the things he had concealed Tom was not a secretive man and he felt alone in his unfamiliar silence. He looked at us several times as if he wanted us to talk, to comment—seeking not so much an idea as an arrange-

ment of words that he could hang on to until his existence could right itself into action.

This fine meditation beautifully describes Tom's subtle inner workings. It is authentic in substance, as it portrays a very believable side of Tom. The problem is in its narrative discontinuity. All of a sudden Nick talks of Tom with the same introspection he uses to talk about himself and Gatsby. But while Nick and Gatsby are the complex conscience of the book, Tom is its physicality: we know him from his gruff speech and big, manly body. Nick has never before considered aloud what makes Tom tick, and he won't again; instead, he places Tom before us as a specimen too automated to analyze. He continually incarnates one thing in the novel—thoughtless machismo. By shading his actions with a peek into his emotional world, Fitzgerald diffuses the power of Tom as a symbol. Despite his symbolic nature, Tom is a credible, living character through action and dialogue, so there was no need to toss in an ill-fitting rumination too. Perhaps realizing this, Fitzgerald deleted the passage.

Continuity, like so much else, is best viewed and repaired when you edit. Lay out the whole manuscript (on a clothesline, wall, or floor) and see how both small details and narrative movements travel like pipelines through the geography of your work. Find the breaks, and if you're editing someone else, point them out; if you're editing yourself, fix them.

SHOW AND TELL

If the theme or plot of your work reveals itself gradually and fully through the action and characters, readers will feel the satisfaction of discovery and new understanding. They will say a silent "ah" at the end, as all the written bits coalesce into a coherent whole. If, however, you dictate your theme or plot through a written PA system, readers will rightfully feel shortchanged. They will hear but not experience whatever point you're making; just as when I was growing up my mother knew that if she told me the meaning of a word, it would go in one ear and, before I experienced it with my own imagination, out the other; whereas if I looked it up myself, I'd interpret and absorb the meaning.

Be careful, then, not to tell your ideas or intentions too much or frequently. Fitzgerald, for instance, showed, didn't tell, what a gruff, macho ditz Tom was:

> I went up to New York on the train one afternoon, and when we stopped by the ashheaps he jumped to his feet and, taking my elbow, literally forced me from the car. "We're getting off," he insisted. "I want you to meet my girl." . . . his determination to have my company bordered on violence. "Hello, Wilson, old man," said Tom, slapping him jovially on the shoulder.

The jump, the taking of Nick's elbow and forcing him from the car, the command instead of an invitation ("We're getting off," not "Would you like to get off with me?"), the jovial slap on the shoulder: these histrionics reveal Tom's character better than any explication.

See if you've told too much or too little, and revise until you find the proper balance. In *Gatsby*, Nick regularly pauses to sum up what is happening and who is at stake. At the start of the book, for instance, he tells us straight out that Daisy's a tricky, insincere snob:

I felt the basic insincerity of what she had said. It made me uneasy, as though the whole evening had been a trick of some sort to exact a contributory emotion from me. I waited, and sure enough, in a moment she looked at me with an absolute smirk on her lovely face, as if she had asserted her membership in a rather distinguished secret society to which she and Tom belonged.

Likewise, Nick's thoughts on Gatsby's fate, part of the novel's coda, tell don't show: "He had come a long way to this blue lawn, and his dream must have seemed so close that he could hardly fail to grasp it. He did not know that it was already behind him." Fitzgerald's use of symbolism makes Nick's explanation far from expository. Gatsby had pursued the green light of money to arrive at a blue lawn of death (death is blue elsewhere in the book: "ghostly birds began to sing among the blue leaves"; "the blue smoke of brittle leaves"). The colors are suggestive, but still mysterious and open to interpretation, especially when read for the first time. Fitzgerald calibrated Nick's ruminations to clarify and emphasize, not spell out the book's meaning.

The point is not to do away with telling, but to edit your explanatory passages until they are well proportioned and well timed. In galleys, for instance, Fitzgerald moved Nick's historical rumination—an aside on the history of Long Island and, in effect, the United States—from chapter one to the book's last page. This straightforward history lesson worked, but had been offered prematurely, letting the thematic cat out of the bag too soon; the reader would have had little to figure out save the plot after that. Structure is a critical ally when you are telling instead of showing: in other words, when to tell is as important as what to tell. When you edit, take note where your reading slows down. Then decide if that section is weak because you are explaining instead of enacting an idea.

BEGINNINGS, ENDINGS, TRANSITIONS

The most important sentence in your work may be the first. With it, you carry the reader out in a verbal undertow—or not. "In my younger and more vulnerable years," begins *The Great Gatsby*, "my father gave me some advice that I've been turning over in my mind ever since." This first sentence prompts us to wonder about a lot: "More vulnerable" than what? Is the narrator invulnerable now, hardened even? What happened to make him so? And what advice would be trenchant enough to turn over in a son's mind for years? A fine beginning often poses a question, or many; but even if it doesn't, it presses the reader—perhaps with the lightest touch—farther into the story. It does this with wit, verbal texture, a syntactic sashay, a vivid setting, an ominous mood, a surprising image, a deeply rooted voice, an offhandedness that says you've entered the middle of a story that began long before you came; or some or all of the above.

What a fine beginning never does is succumb to verbal litter. The simplest and cleanest, such as "I received the following letter," which launches Chekhov's story "The Wife," depend on their clarity and command of voice. Chekhov's beginning also puts us in the middle even at the start. The phrase's immediacy cuts us clean off from our nonreading life and sets us instantaneously in the center of the story, as if we'd been on our way there even before opening the book.

Try this very different launch: "Stately, plump Buck Mulligan came from the stairhead, bearing a bowl of lather on which a mirror and a razor lay crossed." The sentence—the first in James Joyce's *Ulysses*—shimmies and glints. It feels jolly, holy, and a bit unnerving all at once: the words "plump," "Buck," "Mulligan," and "lather" roll in the mouth; even while the mirror and razor "crossed" form a crucifix; and the razor (dangerous in its own right) and glass set atop a filled bowl carried by someone about to walk down a flight of stairs suggests an accident waiting to happen. This is a first sentence that isn't content to only pose questions and foreshadow themes; it wants to be a painting and a fragment of music as well.

The best pulp-fiction writers hone beginnings and endings to their sharpest edge. Surprise and wit, among other things, are in their arsenal. Here are some examples of gripping first sentences: "I am going to kill a man" (Nicholas Blake, *The Beast Must Die*); "They threw me off the hay truck about noon" (James Cain, *The Postman Always Rings Twice*); "I first heard Personville called Poisonville by a red-haired mucker named Hickey Dewey in the Big Ship in Butte" (Dashiell Hammett, *Red Harvest*); "Well, sir, I should have been sitting pretty, just about as pretty as a man could sit" (Jim Thompson, *Pop. 1280*); "Anna Halsey was about two hundred and forty pounds of middle-aged putty-faced woman in a black tailor-made suit" (Raymond Chandler, *Trouble Is My Business*). And though he was not a bona fide pulp writer, it would be a shame to leave out Flann O'Brien's first sentence in *The Third Policeman*: "Not everybody knew how I killed old Phillip Mathers, smashing his jaw in with my spade; but first it is better to speak of my friendship with John Divney because it was he who first knocked old Mathers down by giving him a great blow in the neck with a special bicycle pump which he manufactured himself out of a hollow iron bar." These books all begin with pluck, if nothing else. And though we should not all start off our stories like murder mysteries, we might learn from these genre masters to care more about our first words.

Many writers do not find the first sentence to their book until they edit, because only then, on reading their draft, do they discover that the beginning is hiding on page 3 or 4. They had warmed up for the first few pages, and unwittingly placed the ignition farther in. Recently, I told a student that I thought the beginning of her book was a certain sentence on page 3 and that the first two pages could be largely omitted. She said, "That's the exact sentence that another teacher told me to start with." I took this as affirmation that beginnings are not arbitrary and a good one chimes out even when it's in the wrong place.

We need to think harder about not just the first words of a book or story, but of a chapter, section, or even paragraph that we are writing. Beginnings occur all through our work, again and again. To edit is, in part, to check if each beginning is sound, or if you've allowed in throwaways.

The counterpoint to a great beginning is, of course, a great end. But I am less interested here in the last line of a story or essay, which obviously needs to have flair, than in neglected endings: the last line of a paragraph or chapter. Chandler, for instance, knew how to end his paragraph as wryly as he'd begun it; the one above that catapults fat Anna Halsey into our consciousness ends with: "She said, 'I need a man.' "

Fitzgerald, too, was a master of the squared-off paragraph. He began and ended many with a startling mix of style, philosophy, and itch—the itch that can only be scratched by moving to the next paragraph, but we'll get to transitions in a moment. On page

1 of *Gatsby*, paragraph four begins with the narrator's confession: "And, after boasting this way of my tolerance, I come to the admission that it has a limit." It finishes like this:

> No—Gatsby turned out all right at the end; it is what preyed on Gatsby, what foul dust floated in the wake of his dreams that temporarily closed out my interest in the abortive sorrows and shortwinded elations of men.

Fitzgerald ushers us in and out.

Between all starts and stops are, or should be, transitions; these are the links from one focal point to another in a piece of prose. They can be overt or subtle. An overt transition, for instance, may use the same word in the last line of the preceding paragraph in the first line of the next. Here is a sample of a fine start, finish, and overt transition in the essay "On Morality" by Joan Didion:

> First sentence: "As it happens I am in Death Valley, in a room at the Enterprise Motel and Trailer Park, and it is July, and it is hot."
>
> Last sentence: "With the help of the ice cubes I have been trying to think because The American Scholar asked me to, in some abstract way about 'morality,' a word I distrust more every day, but my mind veers inflexibly toward the particular."
>
> Transitional sentence that begins the next paragraph: "Here are some particulars."

The word "particulars" is an obvious bridge between the first and second paragraphs; between, in other words, her motel-room heat and the story she is about to tell which has nothing to do with that room or heat.

Fitzgerald improved an unsuccessful transition in the scene where everyone drives into Manhattan, Nick, Jordan, and Tom in one car, Daisy and Gatsby in another. Tom is afraid that Daisy and Gatsby will turn off and disappear. In an early draft, Fitzgerald wrote:

> . . . I think he expected them to dart down a side street any minute and out of his life forever.
>
> At the polo grounds we got out and waited—after a blank moment the coupe appeared with insolent leisure around a corner.

In the published book, the same scene reads:

> I think he was afraid they would dart down a side street and out of his life forever.
>
> But they didn't. And we all took the less explicable step of engaging the parlor of a suite in the Plaza Hotel.

The first shift, from "forever" to the polo grounds, is abrupt, the second suave. Not all transitions need to be so direct, but the Didion and Fitzgerald examples demonstrate the beauty and function of a well-considered one.

A verbal transition can be as subtle as the continuation of one idea, without any particular note hitting hard as you move from one prose unit to the next. Subtle is good, obtuse is not. Your reader should not tilt his head, squint, and say "Huh?" because the relationship of one unit to the next is unclear or absent. If a break between sections is needed, but no verbal transition—subtle or overt—makes sense, use a design ornament or a space break to move you through. At the end of the next paragraph you read, for example, you will find a gateway from one style of writing to another: from practical methodology to a summation of purpose.

In short, when you edit, add authority and sway to your beginnings; see if your chapters and paragraphs end with finality; and relate one paragraph to the next.

⌒

To break a text into nameable parts is a ruse—but one that allows us to approach our work in a more organized manner than while we write, which is usually in a state of hypersensitive distraction. Editing gives the writer a chance that writing never will: to see what he is doing. Most of us begin a text, maneuver it, pause. Sooner or later, we reread, realize we are not finished, and then rework it until, again, we pause. Sooner or later, we edit again, again pause; again edit, again pause; and one day we realize that we are not finished, and never will be, but we are willing, if not ready, to stop editing.

It can feel impossible to stop, a feeling that prompted poet Paul Valéry to remark, "a poem is never finished, only abandoned." The danger of ruining a good thing by overediting, then, is ever present. When I go back into my text one too many times, a voice starts to rise in my head, a haunting litany that says, "Don't fix it if it ain't broken." Tolstoy, ruefully admitting to overzealous editing, said, "I strike out what is vivid and replace it by something dull." So after you have been editing your text for a while, leave it alone for a day or a week. When you return, decide if you're done or need to clip just one more word, move just one more section. The problem is that editing is rarely an experience of "just one more" anything.

The only solution is to try hard to hear the editorial wind when it shifts to worsening, not improving, your work. Then stop, undo the last edit, and applaud yourself for having brought your writing to a state of laudable imperfection. "What an editor must fear most," said Max Perkins, "is that he will influence the author too much." When you edit yourself, the same danger exists; the writer in you may be intimidated by the editor in you. If you have the slightest suspicion that you are overediting, you, writer, need to stand up against you, editor.

Self-editing can feel like a war between you and you. I hope these macro and micro chapters will help you end the war, and get on with the work. The macro- and micro-editing lists will not make editing less exhausting, but may make it more efficient and less demoralizing.

Micro-Edit
Diagnostic Checklist

1. **Language:** Language determines that transcendent aspect of a writer's work: her unique style, her voice. Edit out favorite familiar riffs: Kill your shtick.

   a. *Keep language fresh.* Ask: Is this language my own or borrowed? Am I writing new words to fit this moment and this story?

   b. *Keep language precise and concise.* Ask: Is this word or phrase necessary?

      i. Avoid rhetoric that sounds lofty and says little.

      ii. Eliminate verbal filler.

      iii. Avoid adverbs and adjectives. As you edit, ask yourself how this or that sentence reads without them.

      iv. Eliminate tiny words that bog down sentences unless you are using them for a specific purpose (in dialogue, or to achieve a certain rhythm).

   c. *Keep language active.* Make your sentences active and upright. Ask: Have I overused the present participle ("ing" words), especially to modify the verb "to be"? Have I slowed down my prose by using the "standstill" construction, and created monotony by repeating it too many times?

   d. *Keep language real.* Avoid pretentious overwriting. Lyricism can be real, highfalutin rhetoric cannot.

2. **Repetition:** Have you repeated words and expressions? Repetition is only acceptable if there is a reason for it—such as creating a rhythmic pattern, emphasis, or leitmotiv.

3. **Redundancy:** Have you rehashed an idea? If so, keep the more affective expression of it.

4. **Clarity:** Is an idea muddy? A paragraph vague? Have you put three ideas into one sentence, where they are competing with each other and none are clear? Tease them out, and keep them separate in new, simpler sentences. Or structure one complex sentence more carefully.

5. **Authenticity (Image, Dialogue)**: When you edit, make your images ring true. Ask yourself: Does each object mentioned make sense? Make sure your dialogue rings true to your characters and the world you've created. Ask yourself: Do people really say that?

6. **Continuity (Visuals, Character)**: Make sure every aspect of a character is convincing. The tiniest alterations count. Also, keep the visual details straight: A cherry table on page 2 cannot be maple on page 7. In the movie industry, people are hired just to keep visual continuity. Hire yourself to do the same for your text.

7. **Show and Tell**: If you have a traditional plot, did you summarize it, fearful that your reader may not have "gotten it"? Cut out summary. Show what's happening along the way so there is no need for explanation at the end. The point should reveal itself in the action and dialogue.

8. **Beginnings, Endings, Transitions**: All three frequently need to be finessed when we edit. See if the beginning and ending of your sentences, paragraphs, and sections, and of course book, have grace, tension, and purpose.

   As you read, ask yourself if in places you feel abandoned by the author. This may mean that you didn't achieve a smooth or sensible transition; and instead have created a lapse that jolts a reader outside the story.

PRACTICE: THE NOTEBOOK (PERSONAL PATTERNS)

Keep a notebook nearby when you read your own work. Mark down your tics: word repetitions, overused syntactical patterns, a tendency to intellectualize and judge characters, etc. Refer to your log of lapses when you edit. It will help you recognize new instances of old problems.

PRACTICE: PARTNER EDITS

The practice of partner editing improves self-editing because it trains you to see textual details and interpret their effect on a piece of writing. It obliges a clear mind and the clear expression of your editorial ideas.

INSTRUCTIONS

1. Choose a partner—a writer not necessarily working in the same genre or style as you.

2. Exchange a small batch of writing, say five to ten pages.

3. Take your partner's batch home and edit it. Use professional editing symbols (see the appendix "Basic Copyediting Symbols").

4. Exchange your marked-up material with your partner's (you'll be getting your own work back, and he his). Don't discuss what you've done. Take your edited pages home, read them carefully.

5. A day later, meet up, marked-up material in hand, and take turns talking about the edit you've done. You might set a timer for fifteen minutes and start discussing one writer's work; then switch.

6. Do this every week or two, or once a month, for as long as you can or want to. Ideally, you'll get five edits in before you stop or change partners. Keeping the same partner for a while demonstrates the value of trust and intimacy in the editing process.

RULES

1. You may not say, "I love this," "I like this," "This is great," or "I don't like this." These stock phrases offer nothing helpful to a writer.

2. Be precise. Your comments might begin, "This works because . . ." or "This saddened, amused, shocked, or frustrated me," or "I'm confused. What are you trying for here?" or "This character loses depth and individuality in chapter two. He sounds like anybody, whereas in chapter one he is marvelously peculiar. His peculiarity makes him compelling," etc.

3. Be a mechanic, not a judge. When you edit, do not ask yourself: Do I like this? Ask instead: Does this compel me and can I follow it? If the answer is no, figure out why.

4. Be humble. As you read your partner's writing, remember how hard it is for you to write. Do not jump to conclusions about his intention or what needs to be done to make the piece better. Ask questions.

5. Be confident. Trust your instincts. Don't skip a criticism or question because you're not sure you're right. Better to bring it up, even if it ends up unimportant.

6. Speak with equal doses of honesty, clarity, and compassion. Never let your kindness keep you from being straight and thorough. Never let your thoroughness and honesty keep you from being compassionate.

After five editing sessions, discuss with your partner how your editing and self-editing abilities and style may have changed.

Folding It In
Ann Patchett

The moment at which I really feel like I've begun a novel is the day that I sit down and start writing without going back and rereading the thirty pages I've already written. The first two chapters of this book that I'm writing now are like patent leather because I was completely floundering and stuck trying to move onto the third and fourth chapters. I kept going back and polishing.

I think of writing and editing in terms of folding, like you would fold in egg whites. You've got your egg whites beaten and you take a third of them and you lighten the batter by folding it in, and then you take a little bit and you fold it in, you fold it in—I don't feel like writing is linear as much as it is circular. There is this stirring movement of taking the story around in a circle, which means I am always writing back into it.

I'm on page 186 of this novel. So when I went to work this morning I went to work on page 177. I'm trying to write two or three pages a day. There's a really good chance by the time I get to page 186, from page 177, I will have written my two or three pages. Page 186 will become 189. There are also days, because there is a certain stock market quality to all of this, that I'll start on page 177, and when I get to the end, I'll be on page 181 because I will have dumped things. My husband will come and he'll be like, "Are you up or down today?"

⌒

I had an introduction to Bel Canto *that I worked on, I kid you not, for a year. I worked on it for a year because it was so bad. It was so wrong. When I finally finished the book, my friend, who's a writer,*

Elizabeth McCracken, said, "Okay, you have to let it go." With Magician's Assistant, *it was the exact same thing. There was this big opening section that was the last day of Parsifal's life, and Elizabeth said, "You know what?" When I was sixty pages into it, and forty pages was this chunk about Parsifal's birthday, and I had been working on it for a year, she said, "You've got to let this go." And I got off the phone and I sat at the kitchen table and cried. I cried just at the page number, you know? I cried not because I thought it was brilliant or I really thought it should stay in, but because I didn't want to be on page twenty again—and that has got to be the most seventh-grade approach to editing.*

Truth and Beauty [*an account of the friendship between Patchett and writer Lucy Grealy, who died of an accidental heroin overdose*] *had an introduction on it that I worked on for a really, really long time, and it was apologetic and said, for fourteen pages, fourteen different ways, "I was not Lucy Grealy's only friend. This is a story that is just my story, and anybody else could have written this book, and I don't mean to be taking away from anyone else's experience," and I worked so hard on that introduction, and it was all about my guilt, and Betsy Lerner [*Lucy's editor who helped edit Patchett's book*] said, "Just dump it. You don't need any of that." That was such a good piece of advice. I'm so glad that's gone.*

Truth and Beauty *was a book about friendship. And there were maybe three chapters that were interspersed throughout the chronological story that took place after Lucy's death; they were about how I was dealing with her death, and when I finished and I read the whole manuscript, it was just really clear, those weren't interesting to me. They broke the code because Lucy wasn't there anymore. This was not a book about Lucy or me on our own. Also, without Lucy, I did not feel like I was an interesting person at that time in my grief.*

I remember both of my parents, when they read the manuscript of Truth and Beauty, *had a lot of problems with it. My father felt that I had betrayed Lucy because I had painted her in a bad light. My mother felt like I had made myself too vulnerable, and that I would regret letting the public into my life that much . . . I thought, "This is not a project by committee."*

I've got to get the basement right and then build the house. I don't build the house and then change the basement. Once I've got something right I go forward. It is much less a matter of fixing it later on. Is this preemptive editing? Editing for me always happens in the beginning. I guess that's why editors never really work for me.

You Would Need a Crowbar to Get It Out
Scott Spencer

The first draft takes a long time because it's like the teeth of a zipper, each one has to be right for the thing to stay on track. Once a first draft is 300 pages, I've written probably 900. By the time I have a first draft, things are pretty settled. At that point I'm doing the closer work. Then I try to do whatever I can to get some distance from it. Putting it away, if I can stand to, for a month. Reading it in different states of mind. Reading it aloud to somebody; aloud to myself.

The performance aspect of reading out loud can affect the finished product in a bad way: you become sort of pandering. Humor happens when you're writing, it's hard to lay it in afterward because if I'm funny, I'm funny reactively—I need something to bounce off of. Sometimes, after I've finished a draft, I've taken humor out that just sort of trashes what I'm doing. Sometimes the humor is so off—it's just cynical and even sarcastic—that it completely breaks the spell you're trying to cast, whatever contract you've signed with the reader. But then you read out loud, and if a section gets a laugh, you would need a crowbar to get it out.

I've spontaneously changed things around because it just occurred to me, with the stimulation of people there, how to make it funnier. And I'm there literally at the podium with a pen, writing on my manuscript. But a lot of fiction strikes me as having an ingratiating quality that isn't good for the overall book. It comes from how many people read out loud: the professors read at the schools and people read at their writing groups. There is too much of that, because the contact between the reader and the writer is really two people in solitude.

⌒

I've never written more than a sentence at a time without really staring at it and getting up and walking around. I'm not fluid and the trick of editing, or my own self-editing, is to make it feel that it's coming in a flow when the writing is laborious. . . . Anything that can possibly be taken out I try to take out. My books aren't really all that short but I've never wished they were longer. I'd rather wish that someone else wish they were longer.

⌣

I never know if I'm going in the right direction. I think that I'm building a beautiful house and I've built a bus shelter. . . . I find the whole thing very difficult and it's been a sobering experience to find that the fact that I've written eight books doesn't make it easier. In fact, I ask a little bit more of myself each time out. But the lessons of one book don't really give you that clear a map through the next one. Each one has to be invented because each one has its own problems.

But when you edit you ask the same questions for each book. "What can I take out?"—that's my main question.

IV

MASTER CLASS

He is a very complete artist in his own line.
I do not think he will ever acquire the qualities
he lacks but on the other hand he is wholly
master of what he knows.

Eugene Delacroix

Many students come to my class at the New School with the idea that editing is penance for the fun of writing. Or they see editing as a hydra sprouting two new heads for every one that's slain. The trance of writing is far more agreeable to them than the sustained glare of an edit. But if we think about the true nature, not myth, of writing, we'll find that editing is, in some ways, the easy part.

Writing, for instance, is compromised by doubt. We doubt that an astonishing sentence we write is worth an unpaid internship and repeated rejection. Doubt. Writing can be so weighed down by doubt—if not of one's talent then of paying the rent—that it cannot lift off into a trance.

Editing is a different story. By the time we are ready to edit our first draft, we are, in most cases, past the worst doubt, and too invested to give up. A fighting spirit defines and facilitates a good edit. We have put in our time, found (more or less) our purpose, and will not accept defeat. We may sulk after seeing a shoddy draft, but not for long. Life's demands gratefully interfere with self-pity. Soon enough, we will be editing with a vengeance.

And there is this: While we write into a void, we edit into a universe, however ravaged it may be. Editing is to review and to rewrite. To view and write, that is, into what's already written, into a universe we've created, no longer a void. We go back to *something*, not the nothing where we began. The reassurance we feel at having something to work with goes far to explain why editing is, in one important sense, easier then writing: being somewhere is less lonely and frightening than being nowhere. So forget for a minute the intoxication of invention, and honor the cold splash relief of revision.

I cannot furnish a formula for editing, as none exists. Instead, I'd like to offer what has helped me hone my skills: a close look at the work and work process of other artists.

Below, three writers and two artists discuss how they revise their work. I've included artists to offer a fresh view of the writing process. Writers, when looking to learn more about their craft, tend to circle back to the familiar—other writers, other writing tales. A look at artists at work may shake open a writer's calcified idea of editing, and besides, it is fascinating to note the way another vessel navigates the same waters. For we writers and artists are in, while not the same boat, the same creative sea.

Learning about sound editing in film, for example, can jog us into using more careful and creative sound editing when we write. Watching a photographer edit work for a show or a book layout can spark ideas about the juxtaposition of written images. And collaborative editing in the visual arts illuminates the vital balance between being certain and being able to let go of what we were certain of. When we witness editorial collaboration in film and photography, we are also reminded of the need to step outside the creative spell: when we edit, we need to know and say, not just feel, what we want from our work.

Finally, there is the sheer pleasure of watching a master at work. This chapter invites you into the studio of five master editors.

⌒

WALTER MURCH: FILM AND SOUND EDITOR

A film and sound editor of international renown, Murch has edited a slew of movies you've loved or been haunted by or both, including Francis Ford Coppola's *The Conversation*, *The Godfather* movies, and *Apocalypse Now*, as well as the film version of Michael Ondaatje's novel *The English Patient*. A visionary in his field, as well as a technical prodigy, Murch is a Renaissance man whose knowledge of music, art, literature, and science rivals his knowledge of filmmaking, which is encyclopedic. Fortunately, he imparts erudition as naturally as a parent does love.

While watching Murch in action during the making of *The English Patient*, Ondaatje was inspired to interview him in depth about editing. The writer was struck by Murch's deft blending of high technology and poetic vision. The discussion below draws from Ondaatje's series of recorded talks with Murch that resulted in the riveting book *The Conversations: Walter Murch and the Art of Editing Film*. In it, Ondaatje ponders "that seemingly uncrossable gulf between an early draft of a book or film and a finished product."

Most of us take sound for granted. A room is noisy or quiet. We don't stop to think much about the layers of noise we hear or how each noise has a different effect on us. Similarly, when we go to the movies, we think of the soundtrack as the music tacked onto the action. If we comment on a movie's sound, we say, "They killed it with the schmaltzy soundtrack," or when Wim Wenders uses the coolest musicians from all over the world for his films, we say, "Beautiful soundtrack." A soundtrack, though, includes so much more than music. Every chain rattle, car motor, spoon in a cup, gunshot, raindrop, bird wing through the air, and cough are meticulously orchestrated—layered, separated, softened, or intensified—for effect.

Murch makes sound do many things at once: signal a location, create atmosphere, relay a character's psychic world, shock or comfort an audience. Or, when most movies turn sound up to Make Certain You Don't Miss the Dramatic Moment, Murch dares turn it into silence and let the accompanying tension suggest, not pound out, the drama. He uses editing to, among so many other things, rein in his material to let the audience itself connect the dots.

The silence Murch inserted into *The English Patient* is a beautiful example of the tension and texture created by suddenly editing everything away. In a harrowing scene where a Nazi officer interrogates the spy Caravaggio/Willem Dafoe in a closed-off room, the audience hears layers of sound that form a shell around the two men, and by extension the viewers, cranking up their claustrophobia and horror. Outside the room, unseen, a secretary types, a fly buzzes, a telephone rings, a firing squad and soldiers yell. Then, suddenly, when the German officer is ready to act, there is silence.

The sound shelter collapses. Murch has left the audience in a vacuum, shocked by the feeling of time stopped short, and by the unleavened reality before them. It is, as Ondaatje says, a "total and dangerous silence." Then, to make things even more disconcerting, Murch inverts sound and image: just as the officer is committing real violence, he turns the sound on and the image off. Ondaatje explains, "We see nothing violent on the screen. But we *hear* the suggestions of it. And the ones with closed eyes are now under the control of this master editor and so they must imagine it all."

Murch has made an editorial seesaw, with one element up and the other down, then the opposite. Might a writer edit sound and image similarly?

Echoing Fitzgerald's remark on his "intricately patterned" *Gatsby*, Murch explains the gist of his job: "What you do as an editor is search for patterns, at both the superficial and deeper levels—as deep as you can go." Murch's work on *Apocalypse Now*, nothing if not intricate and deep, created, in large part, the film's physical and psychological terrains. He manipulated image and sound to reveal two landscapes—that of the jungle and that of the soldier, Willard's, mind.

Anyone who saw the movie remembers the crickets. Murch added them to the soundtrack to situate us in the jungle. The crickets would have been easy enough to do; he had used that sound in other films and could have laid in the same track he had on file. But regular old crickets wouldn't do here. The sound of them recorded in the normal manner was, explains Murch, "too real, too ordinarily real. We wanted something that was hyperreal . . . [we wanted] a hallucinatory clarity." So Murch recorded individual crickets, and then electronically multiplied them. The recording was not a "shimmering curtain of sound," but rather "as if [the crickets] each had their own little radio mike on." Unmanipulated crickets sound annoying or hypnotic. Murch's manipulated crickets sounded terrifying and other-worldly. A writer might make a similarly nuanced choice of sound to place in a piece of writing. The story's meaning itself, not just its atmosphere, is at stake. Much the way Fitzgerald turned the simple description of Gatsby's face into a nuanced metaphor for his character, Murch used the "hyperreal" crickets to not only indicate location, but as a metaphor for Willard's mental disarray. The crickets stood for the Vietcong that multiplied no matter how many you found and killed, that remained hidden, and that harassed you until you began to lose your mind. "The crickets. . . . Where are they?" says Murch. "They're nowhere. They're in Willard's head. They are spatial, but it's mental space." The lushness of Murch's film editing calls up the tremendous possibilities for editing text. When you edit anything, you are in a position to make each small thing count for more than it appears to be.

Murch also edits with remarkable economy by using what he calls "precipitant sounds": one single, simple noise that brings to the audience's mind something more than itself. In Coppola's *The Rain People*, for example, a woman talks in a phone booth in the pitch black night beside a service station on the New Jersey Turnpike. It is impossible to situate her visually outside the booth. Heavy traffic noise would have indicated a nearby freeway, but would have drowned out the important phone dialogue. Instead, Murch recorded someone dropping a wrench onto pavement in a garage fifty feet away, which was the only sound he put behind the woman's voice. "That little sound," he says, "was able to bring along with it, imaginatively, all the traffic. But the traffic sound exists in your mind. I spend a lot of time trying to discover those key sounds that bring universes along with them." Precipitant sounds evoke the most with the least; they act as literary tropes (metonyms), where one word is shorthand for something connected to it; such as "He was always chasing the nearest skirt," using skirt to mean woman, sex, affairs, and betrayal all in one. In *The English Patient*, precipitant sounds include a tolling church bell that conjures all at once religion, small village life, and the inevitableness of time passing.

Murch's elliptical style would sit well with Milan Kundera, who writes in *The Art of the Novel*: "Encompassing the complexity of existence in the modern world demands a technique of ellipsis, of condensation. Otherwise you fall into the trap of endless length. . . . When you reach the end of a book you should still find it possible to remember the beginning." To edit, as Murch does, is to scrape away extraneous matter that interferes with a story and trust one, well-chosen detail to do the work of ten. It won't hurt a maximalist to ponder Murch's economic use of sound. Would anyone call *Apolcalypse Now* minimal? Even baroque writers would benefit from asking themselves: Would this single image reverberate more if I removed the other images around it? Could this simple descriptive word, placed just so, lead the reader to a new idea, or perhaps several?

～

As an editor, Murch has the courage to be both restrained and rebellious. While working on *The Conversation*, for instance,

Murch would rebel against the original rule of the movie, which was to use a particular line of dialogue as a repeated, strictly unchanging refrain. The story goes that when Coppola ran out of money and time while filming, fifteen pages of the script had not been shot. The set folded. The director then asked his editor to do the seemingly impossible: to edit the incomplete footage into a finished film. To start, Murch had to find editorial Band-Aids for missing scenes. When a park scene, for instance, had no lead-in (no footage of the actors getting to or discussing a trip to the park), Murch turned it into a dream sequence. "Since we had no fabric with which to knit [the park scene] into the reality of the film," Murch says, "it floated for a while, like a wild card, until we got the idea of making it a dream of Harry's. . . . When you have restricted material you're going to have to restructure things from the original intent, with sometimes felicitous juxtapositions." Accidents are for Murch just one more resource.

Early on in the same movie, for instance, an innocuous-looking woman and man talk nervously. The man says, "He'd kill us if he got the chance." The actor emphasizes the word "kill": "He'd *kill* us if he got the chance," which leads the audience to believe that the couple is running for their lives. A surveillance expert named Harry surreptiously records the sentence, and replays it many times in varying circumstances throughout the film. The sentence is a refrain that Coppola uses to question the gap between what we believe is true and what really is. The director decided that the refrain had to remain unchanged throughout the film.

The genteel couple who look innocent, are, in fact, the killers; the "he" in the refrain is a red herring. Murch, as editor, had to make the guilty party clear to the audience without diluting Coppola's point about the ambiguities of perception.

A "mistake" would solve Murch's problem. The editor gleaned his backlog of sound material, with no idea what he was looking for, and came upon a "botched" take of the film's refrain. It had been rejected because the actor had emphasized the word "us": "He'd kill *us* if he got the chance." Murch laid in the botched take at the very end of the film, so that when we hear the refrain for the last time, we are jolted by the fresh emphasis and inescapable meaning: He'd kill *us* . . . so let's kill him first. Aha! The couple was plotting to murder their boss, not the other way around. A mere shift in enunciation changed an entire film. A written story or essay could entirely change from a similar infinitesimal shift.

Murch, in the end, broke the rule to never change the refrain. "Sometimes," the editor concludes, "you can get away with violating your basic premise, which has the effect of throwing the premise into greater relief." What comes clear here is the need to be utterly loose as an editor. Editing is math and editing is also jazz: the editor works within a set equation—the draft and the concept, but she may improvise greatly. It is wise to look through residual material to kindle an idea when stalled. But wisdom alone does not make an editor great. Many editors would look through dross and miss the treasure. Beyond wisdom, an editor has to be hot, inspired, open to the magic of a million-dollar marble lying in the debris.

May Murch provoke us to think harder about sound in writing, and to, as he puts it, "listen to sounds as if they were speech." It is easy to neglect the acoustics of a silent page. Writers who read their work aloud may do better. Dialogue, in any case, can be a bully, and elbow out sounds more delicate than speech. One writer who could create a keen aural world without dialogue was Chekhov. In only one paragraph of the story "The Black Monk," for example, he writes, "From the distance, the violin sounded like a human voice. . . . The whole world seems to be looking at me, has gone silent, and is waiting for me to understand it. . . . He could hear the dull murmur of the pines behind him." That's a good deal of nonverbal sound in one small passage. Chekhov may have appreciated Murch's method, at once esoteric and technical: "Rather than listen to the sound itself, I listen to the space in which the sound is contained."

LUC SANTE: WRITER

With *The Factory of Facts* I became a Luc Sante fan. It is not the book for which he is best known. That one is *Low Life*, a history of Manhattan's seedy side, a book that has garnered a cult following. But the unpredictable and personal *Facts* is my favorite. A "work of remembrance and history," according to its flap copy, it is also a Belgian archaeological dig, a Patinir landscape, a memoir of emigration, a meditation on Euro-American culture, and a part–Sherlock Holmes, part-Camus investigation of Sante's heritage: an investigation that every reader dreams of making for herself and very rarely does.

It is Sante's voice—open, droll, lyrical yet piercingly direct (a bilingual fusion of elastic French and no-nonsense English)—that carries the reader down numerous thematic roads, which all lead to the questions: What is history? What is fiction? What are we if not both? And is it possible to fulfill the catchphrase "make peace with your past"? He writes:

> It is fascinating and often fruitful to try on another skin, but it is ultimately meaningless if one hasn't acknowledged one's own. I already had a history, intriguingly

buried. It might even be an interesting one. Eventually I came to the conclusion that if I did nothing else, I at least needed to uncover it. Maybe some of what I thought was lost was merely hidden.

The euphony of Sante's speech does not come, as I imagined it did, from multiple drafts and rewrites. "I don't do drafts," Sante says. "That is, I don't write it out quickly and then rewrite slowly several times." An interviewer once told Sante that in a pool of more than a hundred writers he had interviewed, Sante was practically the only one to edit the way he does. Most writers exhume their material and later dig through the dirt. Sante does the opposite. He accomplishes the bulk of his dirt sifting even as he writes—in other words, he edits a fair amount in his head. When I suggested to him that his snail's pace took tremendous mental discipline, he scoffed, "I write slowly not because I have the self-control" to keep the pen off the paper, but "because it takes me that long to concentrate." Whether by default or by choice, Sante's slow method recalls Walter Benjamin's dictum: "Keep your pen aloof from inspiration, which it will then attract with magnetic power. The more circumspectly you delay writing down an idea, the more maturely developed it will be on surrendering itself." In more prosaic terms, the riper the idea before it hits the page, the less editing it will need afterward.

But many writers cannot hold back. For them, the sight of words on the computer screen and the feel of their hands tapping a keyboard stimulate the brain, so that they often discover a sentence in the act of writing it. As we tend to admire the thing that eludes us, I admire those who compose largely in the head. No serious writer, however, has it significantly easier than any other.

In the end, writing methods only matter if they hurt your writing: in which case, refer to chapter one. Otherwise, all that counts is the result.

Sante uses the keyboard to perfect, not construct, his phrase. "I write," he says,

> the next paragraph, the next page, painfully slowly, as if I were picking up a transmission from Alpha Centauri on a crystal radio in bad weather. I can't go on to the next sentence until this one feels right—a bit like building a bridge. Things get quicker, usually, past the mid-point mark. And then once I'm done I tinker endlessly.

A fierce micro-editor, Sante macro-edits very little. At the end of a work, he allows himself free-fiddle with words but not structure. For Sante to change or move a word has structural ramifications. "Editing," he says, "has to do with words. But word choice is more than just a question of precision; the change of a word can completely reorient the meaning. The inaccessible word, when suddenly accessed . . . can suggest an entirely new avenue to drive down."

Sante listens incredibly hard to his own words, until they convey the direction needed, and this careful forward movement naturally forms the structure. Sante's respect for the subconscious path of a narrative echoes the Surrealists, whom he read early on and who, he muses, may have influenced his editing technique. "I rarely cut and paste . . . I work strictly in sequence, and while I've deleted many pages of things, I've rarely moved paragraphs or sections around. . . . This is my version of 'first thought, best thought.'"

That Sante avoids the classic cut-and-paste does not mean

structure comes easily to him. With *Facts*, he admits, "the structure nearly drove me around the bend. I had no idea how to harness this huge mass of stuff." He tried, at his wife's suggestion, a flow chart on a twelve-foot-long piece of paper tacked to a wall with color-coded notations. The chart, which would have worked for many writers, got him nowhere.

At last, he tried a trick he'd used on previous books: he wrote down chapter titles and figured out "what stuffing would match." He refers to this method—a systematic matching of content to title—as an intervention on the part of his "best editor, the subconscious mind." The result is a book where myriad themes move about in a pretty simply shaped room. No complex infrastructure apportions or funnels divergent topics, as if to say, "Life is not so neat and carefully segmented, shouldn't writing reflect this prism?" The setup creates occasional thematic congestion, but also marvelous conjunctions of thought and feeling that would never occur in a more strictly ordered setting. In one chapter, for instance, Sante starts with a funny riff on birthdays and the rivalry he felt, as a boy, with others who shared his own. From here, he smoothly segues to Belgium in 1954, the year of his birth. Several pages later we come to the following description of his mother walking down a street, that same year, in his Belgian hometown of Verviers:

> As my mother, *filet a provisions* in hand, negotiated her way through the aisles of La Vierge Noire in the direction of the leeks, a grocer nasally trilling something about *toutes ces fleuuuuurs*—maybe a congealed Tino Rossi—and somebody else just outside the door barking a mechanically repeated phrase so elided that you could just make out the single word *tombola*—lottery—and the one-two bells of

the streetcars and the deliberate deep bells of Notre-Dame des Recollets all colliding, my grandmother waited outside with me, half-dozing in my pram, dressed too warmly for August, probably, but you never knew when a sudden breeze might come up.

Structural logic is not forsaken, but scrupulously integrated into Sante's flinty voice, which coaxes us to follow him wherever matters most. With "probably" near the end, Sante continues to unpack his overall intention to question the veracity of memory. For all the care he takes, Sante says he is

proceeding . . . blindly. The better the writing is going the less I'm able to account for what it is I just did. Sometimes—and this is when writing becomes miraculous, even for an atheist—I get the next sentence dictated to me, which means, generally, that I hear its exact rhythm before I know what the words will be that compose it.

Sante's writing in his head reminds me a little of Judith Freeman's writing by hand. For both, to write slowly makes their editing go faster, as their work is in rather fine shape at the end of the first, carefully rendered draft.

In 2003, Sante edited a new afterword for *Low Life*. He cut the originally published afterword down from seven thousand to four thousand words. Sante, true to his nature, did not cut and paste. He deleted whole pages and worked to gracefully close up the gaps. He "didn't actually move anything," he says, but tightened what existed in its original order. If you're wondering what it might mean to lose three thousand words in one fell swoop: "the result," says Sante, delighted if a bit dazed by the magnitude of his edit, "is far superior to the original."

While many self-editors walk this earth with an invisible scissors in hand, ready to transpose or trim if given the chance, Sante has no inclination to edit extensively on the back end of a draft. He edits it from the front, and proves that there is no single right way to edit.

MITCH EPSTEIN: PHOTOGRAPHER

Collected by major institutions such as New York's Museum of Modern Art and the Whitney Museum of American Art, Mitch Epstein's photographs bring to mind a marriage of Edward Hopper and Jean-Luc Goddard for their narrative complexity, color wisdom, and wit. Though they are made in the world, not a studio, their iconic quality feels constructed as well as serendipitous. Epstein looks for ordinary things that may, he says, through being photographed "take on a metaphorical charge." A dusty briefcase on a floral mattress, a fluorescent rod set vertically against a pink wall, a lone elderly couple driving golf balls on an enormous range become, in Epstein's pictures, more than themselves, become mythic.

For Epstein, editing is pivotal and he engages in it at several stages of creation. He edits the picture frame while photographing; edits a batch of pictures into a select few; edits the sequencing and layout of his pictures for presentation in an exhibition or publication. This last edit has traditionally been left to picture editors, art directors, and curators: the photographer hands over his pictures to one of these professionals who figures out how to present them in a magazine, book, gallery, or museum. Although Epstein doesn't always have the last say with magazines, which discourage artists from entering the editing process, he now hands over a very careful preliminary edit to persuade the official editor to present the work according to his vision of it. It wasn't always this way. Epstein used to, like most photographers, leave it to "the experts" to edit his pictures for the public.

Epstein goes so far as to define what he calls his "artistic maturation" as the ability to edit. His celebrated teacher, Garry Winogrand, had a manic passion for shooting pictures, but little interest in editing them. He left, after his death, tens of thousands of images unwinnowed, unorganized; and a legacy of athletic prowess for making a photograph and impatience with what to do with it afterward. Epstein absorbed this legacy.

During the early years, after a shoot, Epstein did what amounted to a quick one-shot review: look, choose, shoot more, look, choose, shoot more, and so on. Perhaps he unconsciously knew that he was giving his editorial process short shrift, because he kept his so-called rejects and stored them in boxes for decades. Eventually, for his retrospective book, he would painstakingly edit what amounted to twenty thousand images, and, sure enough, find a good deal of gold left in with the grit. When we are young we see our work differently from when we are older, and sometimes the long wait to edit serves an artist well. It gave Epstein time to intellectually catch up with what he had done intuitively as a young man.

It is advisable, then, not just to edit more slowly the first time around, but to keep anything you suspect might later have value. Writers do well to keep a file of their most intriguing unused sentences and insights. Journals fulfill this function in a random fashion, but a more organized filing of your literary bits—with files fashioned after photographic archives, tabbed, for instance, character, landscape, dialogue; or the body, the sea, animals, painting, etc.—could also be useful during an edit when you're looking for a specific something to torque up your text.

Midway into his career, Epstein reconsidered how much power he gave to professional editors to choose the size, juxtaposition, placement on a page or wall, and background color for his pictures. World politics, strange as it may sound, helped make him a more self-sufficient editor.

From 1992 to 1995, he, an American, spent time in Vietnam, where politics ruled his daily life. Watched over by Communist agents who followed him and intercepted his letters, Epstein began to think more about the locus and mechanics of power. He had been collaborating on a book with a dissident writer who one day told him that in order to continue working together he'd have to submit his pictures to the Vietnamese government for censorship. Epstein broke the collaboration instead. *Vietnam: A Book of Changes* was published with the photographer's own text, but the experience shook him: it challenged his view of the power, not just of Communist apparatchiks, but curators, art directors, editors, and the media, to recast his vision. Too many strangers, however well meaning, had been tampering with the artwork that Epstein knew most intimately; he knew now he would need an outside second look, but that the first long and hard one had to be his own. "Conquering that [censorship] dilemma gave me the cue to take responsibility for how my work was edited and presented," he says. "It was about taking control. Editing is about having power over your work."

Art books have long delighted Epstein as the most democratic art venue and as a complex formal challenge. He has now made six of his own, and the photography book has become his second art. His books are not image banks so much as visual novels that he edits with three main things in mind: the instantaneous effect of a single image; the dynamic between two or more images across a spread; and the gaining force of a carefully built, if abstract, narration from a book's beginning to its end.

The book *Family Business*, a chronicle of the demise of his father's furniture store and real-estate dynasty, showcases everything careful editing can do right, such as create momentum, tension, mystery, humor, and meaningful questions. The book's innovative form (it uses video stills, text, and photographs) "resulted from a protracted, intensive editing process as much as anything else," says Epstein. "I try to pair pictures so they won't succumb to obvious literal associations. The strongest work is ruthlessly clear and simple and yet open to a vast range of interpretation." In *Family Business*, for instance, the artist placed an image of snow-covered branches on the right page, and facing it, on the left, a vintage slot machine set on a workbench in a sloppy suburban basement—the machine tells your fortune for a nickel with questions written across it: "Will I be a big shot?" "Does she love me?" "Will she let me drink?" The two images appear to have nothing in common, but somehow look destined for one other. Asked about that pairing, Epstein avoids easy explanations: "The quality in that juxtaposition is not easily nameable. That's the beauty of it." When pressed, Epstein admits to certain correspondences:

> interior/exterior; the absence of color versus the fullness of color; the chaos of my father's no-longer-functional-workbench is a history of human life filled with promise, joy, and disappointment versus the trees adorned with fresh snow, a picture that, while it may have human associations,

is to me much more simply about what you see: how that backyard looks after a virginal snowfall. One may conjure ideas of innocence, fresh possibility, but such readings can be foolhardy. The pairing may work just because one picture is vertical and the other horizontal; or one is red and the other white!

Epstein's warning is well taken. But when you edit, you must justify your decisions—to a collaborator if you have one, but most of all to yourself. Artists and writers love to say their best work happens when they don't know what they're doing. But unknowing is only a first step; the next, during the editing process, is to know. Editing insists that the artist and writer figure out (for the most part) what they did, even if they will never know how they did it. When you edit, it will rarely do to say, "I just like it this way." *Why* do you like it this way?

Often, it isn't until you explain your views aloud that you understand them. Collaboration is generally unnatural to writers—most would put solitude ahead of cash if asked to choose between the two. But collaboration suits people who work in music, theater, and cinema. Perhaps because Epstein has worked in film as a production designer, cinematographer, and producer, he has come to value an exchange of ideas at propitious moments during the months, sometimes years, he spends creating a photographic body of work. With this in mind, he asked me and another colleague, printer/photographer Christoph Gielen, to help him edit a museum show of *Family Business*. Our experience together points up how important it is for an artist to hold equally in mind two seeming opposites when he edits: certainty and flexibility. In the following account, Epstein's ability to not give up on an idea he was sure of and yet be open to a new interpretation of it offers a fine model for self-editing.

After he'd made his plan and chosen the pictures to fill it in, Epstein called Gielen and me over to see. The museum was in an old converted power station that had one large room with three walls (the fourth had a huge window). Epstein chose to place landscapes and still lifes on two walls, and four large portraits on the third. Each portrait would represent a different part of his father's world: Bill's Puerto Rican tenant, a Polish fireman he knew, his ox-strong bookkeeper of fifty years, and his bourgeois wife. The idea was that together, the portrait wall and the two walls of environmental imagery would re-create his father's universe, while Bill himself would not show up here, since he would be the center of attention in two videos set downstairs.

This concept was inspired and sound, and the pictures Epstein chose worked very well—except one. The image of Bill's wife, Ruth, was not as powerful as the other three. "But we need her as a counterbalance to the others," Epstein said, "and this is the best one I have." But the picture wasn't good enough. I argued that the artist should not sacrifice the quality of his show for the beauty of his concept. Epstein, in turn, explained why a picture of Ruth had to stay on that wall: she represented something in Bill's life that no one else could. For one, she was—with her upper-middle-class elegance—a socioeconomic contrast to the others. She was also Bill's single intimate refuge. Her portrait, though weak on its own, was a vital piece of the whole. Gielen agreed that the photograph of Ruth fell short. We were at an impasse. Epstein looked sorry he'd ever asked for anyone else's opinion, but now it was too late.

To move things along, Gielen and I talked through our precise reasons for disliking the image. We made a verbal list: *It's static;*

Ruth's body is incidental instead of expressive; her face is complex but her eyes look absent; her beige clothes reinforce the neither-here-nor-thereness of the picture; the background (a suburban road) is unresolved—too far to be an interesting texture, too close to be a meaningful environment. Because we'd stopped giving vague impressions such as "I don't like it" or "It just doesn't work," Epstein listened harder to us and finally agreed that the picture had to go.

What to put in its place? We tried using superb portraits of other people: a city councilman, a tenant, the family housekeeper. The effort, however, only proved Epstein's original point. Nothing made sense in that spot except for Ruth.

We were now in an editorial stew: I had convinced Epstein of my view and he had convinced me of his—we were further along, and had gotten nowhere.

On the third day, after having tried several more portraits, we sunk into collaborative despair. Then, to my and Gielen's shock, Epstein put the missing picture up for grabs. He asked us, "If you could put anything in that spot, what would you put? *Anything at all.*" The picture we needed was destined for a portrait wall, but now we were free to think beyond portraits. It was awkward at first. One hundred fifty images hung as thumbnails on a bulletin board: landscapes, still lifes, street pictures, scenes of domestic life, and portraits. We scanned them.

Gielen pulled out a picture of the seventy-year-old housekeeper, Fran, but this time *not a portrait*. Here, Fran stood outside Bill's house with a hose in her hands, spraying a birdfeeder on a high branch. Shot from behind a picture window, the water sprayed toward the camera and gave the illusion of getting the viewer wet. Fran's elderly body bent back like something brittle barely managing not to break. It was good. Very good. Yet after a few minutes we shook our heads: as much as we wanted it to be, this picture simply didn't fit.

I found myself staring then at an image of Ruth lying on a white wicker love seat, her eyes focused on the ceiling. A cheerful watercolor hung on the wall above her and a matching wicker lamp stood at her feet. Amid these ordinary objects of her suburban home, Ruth lay in a trance. Her bent knees formed a triangle in the center of the image, which both anchored the picture and gave it a kinetic tension. It was a strange and powerful photograph, but not a portrait. Epstein thought it was too different from the others. None of us thought it would work. But when we held it next to the other three portraits, there was no question that it did.

Epstein's concept was fulfilled now, but only after it had bent to accommodate a novel idea: nonportraiture. We had intended the wall to hold traditional August Sander–like portraits. But this eccentric photograph of Ruth complemented the three other traditional portraits perfectly; positioned last, Ruth appeared to be dreaming the people next to her, dreaming, as it were, her and Bill's life.

I learned a good deal from the above episode. Epstein had rightly insisted on his concept. By holding me in his conceptual pen for as long as he did, he trained my brain, when the gate opened, to go for the variant of Ruth, rather than abandon her altogether. Conversely, Gielen, by being loose, got me to loosen up. I might have remained stuck on traditional portraits had Gielen not seen beyond portraiture before I did.

Forget about being pure. As Murch did with the refrain "He'd kill us if he got the chance" in *The Conversation*, Epstein cheated on a concept to fulfill it. He carefully balanced his autonomy with an open mind: mental acrobatics any editor of any medium could stand to learn. Purists are people who create ideas, not art. At some point, when you work with an editor, she will say you have erred, and you will have to somehow blend her insights with your own. Sometimes everyone is right, yet each with a blind spot. We need, as Epstein did, to maintain our authority even as we open up to an opposing point of view.

MARY CAPONEGRO: WRITER

An avant-garde stylist of hair-raising finesse, Mary Caponegro is a master of the short story. Engineered almost as intricately as DNA, her stories (*The Complexities of Intimacy, The Star Café*) are as hilarious as they are deep, and often dark. Plot is not, as Caponegro puts it, "in the foreground" of her work. Her stories brim, however, with human drama. The dramatic tension comes in part from the reader's discovery of "what happens next," but also, largely, from the author's linguistic stringencies and sentiment-shredding satire.

"The Father's Blessing," for instance, satirizes a maniacal priest who has just married a young couple and refuses to extricate himself from their lives:

> Because I am a sincere man I must tell you that there is indeed advantage to the closet called confessional: one can be so close, intimate; only a thin screen separates oneself from the sinner, one's own sagacious voice from the whispers which reveal the deepest secrets. That is our special privilege; one might say power: that no one can justify surprise or suspicion when I appear on the other side of, by extension, any partition. There is, with me, potentially greater intimacy than that between a man and wife: one

bound to breed resentment, foster ambivalence; for people
are uncomfortable robbed of accusations . . .

The sibilance of this paragraph sounds out secrecy itself:
Caponegro has managed to linguistically embody—in a paragraph-
long whisper—the invasions of the Catholic Church on a person's
intimate life. The hard *c* of "closet," "called," "confessional,"
"close," "uncomfortable," and "accusations" plays off the predom-
inant sibilants (and similar *sh*, *ch*, and soft *g* sounds), which,
alone, would be too cute: an alliterative cliché. Instead, due to
careful balancing and a sharp purpose, the slithering *ss* work.
Read the paragraph over just to hear the music of the *s*, *ch*, *sh*, and
c notes. Caponegro makes meaning and language merge until
they can't be told apart.

Caponegro's unusual style has not been easy for traditional
readers to edit. She has undergone hardships, along with good
fortunes, with various editors over the years, all of which taught
her to rely most on herself as an editor, even while she remains
open to the counsel of a select few.

When she was beginning as a writer, editing first appeared in
the guise of teaching. At university, "The tutelage of mentors,"
Caponegro says, "was a huge part of my artistic growth." There
were novelists Robert Coover and John Hawkes and the poet
Robert Kelly; the latter worked with Caponegro, "word-by-word
on the page" she says, "as part and parcel of the larger vision they
knew was mine." *Conjunctions* editor Bradford Morrow provided a
bridge between mentorship and commercial editing.

After she left school, teaching and editing became two separate
activities. "When you're working with teachers you're working with
process," Caponegro says. "The difference with a bona fide editor is

you're no longer working with process. To some degree sometimes that does come into play, but mostly it's to get that product to be the most polished artifact it can be." Faced with the pressures of the book industry, a professional editor, then, is less pedagogue, there to help you investigate all the possibilities to enact your vision, and more personal trainer, there to diminish your narrative sags.

Caponegro had the good fortune, though, to enter the mainstream of book publishing with John Glusman (then executive editor of Collier Books and senior editor of Charles Scribner's Sons) as her editor. He bought her first book, *The Star Café*. His manner, she says, was neither cuddly nor cold, but "kind and businesslike." Glusman's consummate professionalism won her:

> I remember how different it felt that somebody was looking at my work with an eye for making it a little bit more accessible. It was disconcerting at first to have someone saying, "Do you really need that sentence to be that long? Can we make three sentences out of it?" I had been given such license to be excessive; there was something really refreshing and educational in John's edit. It was a turning point. There was somebody who had a completely different perspective but didn't seem hostile and could accommodate my vision. John wanted to make it more accessible but not to dumb it down, not to compromise it in a way I couldn't tolerate.

With Glusman's help, Caponegro matured as a published writer. He was not, as she put it, "one of the avant-garde family members that said, 'yes, you're fighting the good fight; we're in the same camp' "; but his ginger touch with her work bespoke his respect for it and allowed her to trust him.

There were, in fact, benefits to his being an outsider: Glusman helped Caponegro gain independence and distinguish herself from her pack. The umbrage of former teachers and literary stewards was vital to Caponegro's writing life. That said, by leaving her literary home to face editing ideas different from hers and her mentors', she kept fresh and agile. Her willingness to listen to new and opposing views of how to edit her work recalls Walter Murch's rule of continually working with new assistants. "I enjoy the variety—I thrive on it, actually," he says, "not only because new people bring new ideas but also because *I* have to redefine, reexamine *myself* and my sometimes hidden assumptions. How do I work? Why am I making certain choices? Is that really the best way to do it?" Sometimes empathetic outsiders, more than insiders with an aesthetic agenda, can help us better understand what we are doing and why.

Now, some twenty years later, Caponegro's apprenticeship is long past. She relies mainly on herself to edit. The experience of being edited helped her edit herself: after working with her mentors, Caponegro trusted her untraditional instincts when she was alone. And the reexamination of her own assumptions that Glusman encouraged is something she continues to do on her own.

It is fascinating to see how her self-editing has changed from her early writing years. Formerly possessed by the harmonics of a story, Caponegro tries harder now to balance harmonics with clarity. Describing how she used to edit herself, she says,

> I'd always write out loud. When I got that opening, I would repeat it out loud, over and over and over . . . because it was so important to me that the sonic qualities were intact in every single line. A lot of my self-editing would be

preoccupied with trying to maintain the standard in my head of musicality. In the last five years, I have understood that this might be a liability. I wanted to make writing so beautiful that my editing was really about going over every single syllable so that it matched up in my head with some paradigm, some Platonic idea of the music of prose. I would go over it for clarity too, but I would always sacrifice clarity for what I considered a poetic achievement of the line.

Caponegro's singular method has given and still gives her prose a symphonic beauty. But now, the philosophical and emotional blood of a story flows closer to the narrative skin.

When she needs a fresh perspective, Caponegro shows her work to Michael Ives, whom she lives with and who also happens to be a writer. "The toughest editor I've ever had is Michael," she says. "He looks for clarity so scrupulously. Any word that seems off, any idea that seems like you have to give it the benefit of the doubt, any clause that's a little floppy, he is just ruthless." His concern for clarity coincides with Caponegro's desire to move beyond the lushness she has already mastered. "Now," she says, "I want to be looking more toward restraint."

At its best, editorial conversation, just as any passionate intellectual exchange, gilds a romance. It has for Caponegro and Ives, but as for so many artist couples the beginning was not altogether easy. "As a teacher," says Caponegro, "encouragement had always been for me the most crucial part of editing; but Michael looked at editing very detachedly." Caponegro wanted Ives to reassure her before he picked a story apart. Ives figured his love for the piece was a given, why waste time repeating it when there was work to be done?

Caponegro and Ives were at an impasse and stopped editing

each other for a while. When they eventually began to read each other again, their editing dialogue was different: "He's gentler now and I'm more receptive," she says. "Talking about the work has a lot to do with the growth of the relationship. We learned how to be more sensitive to each other's needs, but also be more receptive to the truth and the rigor that was in each other's comments."

Solo editing can benefit from the lessons we learn with our partner. We can become, for instance, more "sensitive" to our own vulnerability and, at the same time, toughen ourselves to our own critiques.

MAURICE BERGER: WRITER

White Lies tackles the racial confusion we all get handed as an American legacy. It mostly sidesteps the country's obvious bigots: extreme right-wingers and neo-Nazi punks. Instead, it targets educated white liberals (like the author himself) who live under the illusion they are prejudice-free. The most progressive whites, Berger shows, are walking palimpsests of racial fear, suspicion, estrangement, and disdain. He asks readers to acknowledge this truth as a first step to revamping it.

Berger, a curator, teacher, and culture critic who specializes in race issues, has been writing and publishing for twenty-five years. But for most of those, he claims, he did not understand editing. "It's only in the last year that I've learned how to edit myself," he says.

It was, in part, the switch to writing a book, after having written only essays, that woke Berger up to the value of scrupulous self-editing. The leap from individual essays to book-length narrative can be daunting. The essayist must suddenly learn endurance; and while he used to hand his text to a magazine or newspaper that employed a staff of editors to do nothing but tidy up his writing, now he must tidy it up himself. For the former magazine writer, the book is on one hand a luxury—with its ample time for reconsidering every word and idea—and on the other a trap, where the sudden freedom to edit the hell out of your manuscript leads you to endless, out-of-control fussing.

Berger eased his transition by writing *White Lies* as a pastiche of short, self-contained vignettes in alternating voices (Berger's, friends' and colleagues', and literary excerpts)—one to six pages long. While there were other reasons for the fragmentary form that we'll get to later, the pastiche proved a useful entry to book-length narrative.

Composed entirely of fragments, then, the book posed particular editing problems. With so many small bits to assemble, it was easy to skid away from the central point. Berger's publisher at Farrar, Straus & Giroux, Jonathan Galassi, helped streamline the work. "Galassi's edits," Berger says, "pushed me to make the vignettes shorter and stick to the point. I couldn't always tell what information wasn't necessary. But he could." The author recalls,

> John would say, "don't veer off into tangents when you use the paratactic form. You're giving the reader a minimal amount of information to begin with, let the information be about the subject of the vignette; let the vignette be about the subject of the book strictly." So if I would talk about quirks my parents had that had little or no bearing on the issue of their racial attitudes, Jonathan would say, "I think you're better off not going there."

Aided by Galassi's edit, *White Lies* achieved the steady concentration of a sonnet.

In fact, Berger had not planned to use the paratactic form. In the epilogue, he writes:

> I search through my files for the original proposal for the book. . . . As I read . . . I am surprised at its almost adolescent assuredness, its steadfast belief that white racism can be conquered. The proposal calls for a rather substantial book, linear in its argument and organized into five neatly defined chapters. Instead, I see now I have written the book in fragments.

Berger discovered along the way, he says, that he wanted his narrative form to mirror "the contradictions and ambivalence of a conversation on race; I wanted a form to reflect the anxiety and disjunction of racism." Here again is an artist wisely abandoning a preconceived ideal to let his material guide him.

Today Berger no longer writes in fragments, a form that can, he says, become a crutch. He was about to use it for a new book when Galassi said, "Maurice, the vignettes worked for *White Lies*, there was a reason you used them for that book. But don't do it anymore. Because you really do know how to write and your greatest art will come when you speak simply and narratively and you let yourself talk for a while."

After thinking "this is a nightmare," Berger began to rethink the nature of linear nonfiction narrative. Having worked for a long time among academics whose jargon-choked, belligerent prose he loathed, he had feared if he wrote long, he'd write like them. Now he saw another way, and was confident in his ability to edit his prose to fit his vision. "Authority doesn't have to be so commanding that it doesn't leave room for questions," he says. With careful editing he knew now that he could control his writing instead of his reader, whom he merely wanted to guide.

Galassi had encouraged Berger "to get more personal, a little less analytical" in *White Lies*. Yet it is hard to enter a nonfiction text personally without invading it. It is during the edit that the writer can see where she has let out a self-absorbed drone and where her self-revelation is linked to a theme in her work. The question to ask is: Are you just talking about yourself or talking about yourself as a stepping-stone to an idea?

Berger's account in *White Lies* about a subway ride from his boyhood, for instance, shows how a writer can be personal without being aimlessly confessional. He and his friend Kevin, who is black, argue about the television show *All in the Family*. Kevin likes the show's honesty, while Berger espouses the white liberal's knee-jerk objection to overt racism. Berger writes:

> Just as Kevin began to change the subject, a middle-aged black woman tapped me on the shoulder. "Let me tell you something, young man," she said. "White people really hate it when racism is thrown back in their faces. White people can be so ugly and stupid. You're not worried about *All in the Family* making racism acceptable. What really worries you is that Archie's racism might look a whole lot like your own."

> Her comment confused me. It embarrassed me. It made me want to tell her I wasn't a bigot. Instead, I said nothing, relieved that my best friend was as reluctant as I to take this conversation any further.

Following Galassi's advice and his own instincts, Berger edited himself more into his book; and made sure his presence served the overarching theme.

The concept of editing, which Berger had taken for granted, began to fascinate him during and after his work on *White Lies*. He recalls, with nearly religious fervor, the edit he received from an independent editor, Anna Jardine, on a recent essay: "Repetitions were deleted or questioned; unnecessary words were deleted; rhythms that were slightly off were made more elegant and less awkward. [Anna] had a keen sense of what I was trying to do as a writer, not just an intellectual."

Editors Galassi and Jardine, as well as Paul Elie—whose micro-edit of *White Lies* Berger describes as "elegant"—offered meticulous editorial surveillance that might have made Berger lazy and increasingly reliant on them. Instead, he took their example and began to rely more on himself:

> Something profoundly important happened to me as a writer. My father used to quote a biblical saying, "if I am not there for myself, who will be for me?" Very slowly, I have learned to be my own best editor. I love to be edited. But I've learned to see where I repeat myself over and over again, where I use awkward words, where I use unnecessary sentences.
>
> It's much harder for me to write now, it takes much longer. The writing process has become quite painful, but the pain results in feeling I've ended up with something I'm happy to publish. The pain results in the bizarre experience of having editors send essays back with almost no changes.

For Berger, the strain of editing is worth the new satisfaction he feels when he has finished writing.

⌒

To master editing is for many to become a master, and it often takes time. In the thirty-seventh year of her career, famed choreographer Trisha Brown had an epiphany during a performance: "I knew, at that moment, the long haul of my apprenticeship in choreography was over." Thirty-seven years it took to feel she had mastered the alchemy of technique, inspiration, and vision. The full importance of editing comes late to many artists and writers, such as Mitch Epstein and Maurice Berger who figured out its tremendous value after years of trying to minimize it. Mary Caponegro, however, was weaned on it. Luc Sante values it almost despite himself, and Walter Murch, long conscious of what he is doing as a professional editor, has turned it into an extraordinarily creative science. Editing is what lets them all roam freely inside the creation of their art, knowing they will at some point come up against an aesthetic fence, a technical wall, an emotional door. Editing forces them to decide whether to accept the obstacle or go beyond it. Editing forces them to look at a problem in their work, and solve it. Editing creates a crucial system of questioning for these artists; and they know their work will not be done until they've answered the toughest questions.

As Though Sound and Sense Were One and the Same
Harry Mathews

*When I wrote my first novel, any ideas I may have had about editing
were vague to the point of nonexistence. I was probably too thrilled by
having produced a book to realize that there is always room for
improvement. I was gently introduced to the possibility by Berenice
Hoffman and Maxine Groffsky at Random House. But it was also
true that this novel had largely "written itself," and not all that many
changes were necessary.*

*It was very different with my next three books. They all needed
considerable rewriting, and I gradually became aware of editing as a
job to be done on different levels—perhaps they could be called local,
transitional, general? I've never worked out what's required methodically enough to devise a precise vocabulary; but certainly thorough
editing has to attend to the details of writing, to the continuity
between paragraphs, chapters, and other divisions of a book, and to
the overall proportions of the work. Doubtless there are other things to
do as well. Continuity may elude definition but it's so important—
the drama and very life of prose. (Think of what happens between
chapters and sections in Austen, James, and Ford Madox Ford.
Between sentences in Chandler and Jane Bowles.)*

In the case of Cigarettes *I benefited from having my ex-wife Niki
de Saint Phalle read the first drafts—she was a very perceptive reader,
and tough, too: she gave me a very hard time, and rightly so, since
those two drafts were pretty awful. After that I had the immense good
fortune of working with Mark Polizzotti, then an editor at Weiden-*

feld & Nicolson. I had already completed two sentence-by-sentence rewrites of the novel and felt I'd done quite enough; Mark asked me five questions about it that wholly re-engaged me in the editing process and prompted me to make a number of substantial modifications of the text. I can't recall [what the five questions were]. They worked wonderfully as catalysts and were quickly forgotten as soon as I'd gotten back inside the novel.

An editor should have a flair for understanding what an author is doing in a particular work. This sounds obvious, but it's worth remembering that sometimes authors themselves aren't altogether clear—at least intellectually clear—about their aims, which often reveal themselves only as the writing is done. If he has this flair, an editor should then firmly make clear what in the novel or story is getting in the author's (and the reader's) way. I guess the editor can sometimes even suggest a solution to a particular problem, but the best approach is to nudge the author into a position where he is willing and eager to solve it himself.

⌒

I try to remember always to read what I've written out loud: that shows up local mistakes effectively. Otherwise I start by cutting out what's obviously not essential, and then what I thought was necessary but turns out not to be, and that process goes on and on—it sometimes seems that the only way I know a piece is finished is when I've removed the last of my favorite (but, alas, expendable) details. So I suppose that for me the main part of editing is cutting. (The second draft of the book I'm now working on was one third shorter than the first.) What matters most is to get the sentences right, one after the other; they have to ring true, as though sound and sense were one and the same.

I do only routine revision in the course of writing, and I never reread what I've written until I've completed the current draft of the entire work: I feel that if I reread as I went along I'd never get past page one.

V

SERVANTS, DICTATORS, ALLIES: A BRIEF HISTORY OF EDITORS

But who shall be the master? The writer or the reader?
Denis Diderot, *Jacques le Fataliste*

"The function of an editor," Gardner Botsford, then editor emeritus at *The New Yorker*, once told me, "is to be a reader. Really, that's all it entails." He swiped the air with his hand to preempt the fuss I might make about what he did for a living. Reading is important, "every writer in the world needs somebody to read the stuff before it's published," but not *that* important, he implied, and certainly less so than writing.

Botsford's noble modesty, however, misrepresents the real work of an editor. An editor doesn't just read, he reads *well*, and reading well is a creative, powerful act. The ancients knew this and it frightened them. Mesopotamian society, for instance, did not want great reading from its scribes, only great writing. Scribes had to submit to a curious ruse: they had to downplay their reading skills lest they antagonize their employer. The Attic poet Menander wrote: "those who can read see twice as well." Ancient autocrats did not want their subjects to see that well. Order relied on obedience, not knowledge and reflection. So even though he was paid to read as much as write messages, the scribe's title cautiously referred to writing alone (*scribere* = "to write"); and the symbol for Nisaba, the Mesopotamian goddess of scribes, was not a tablet but a stylus. In his excellent book *A History of Reading*, Alberto Manguel writes, "It was safer for a scribe to be seen not as one who interpreted information, but who merely recorded it for the public good."

In their fear of readers, ancients understood something we have forgotten about the magnitude of readership. Reading breeds the power of an independent mind. When we read well, we are thinking hard for ourselves—this is the essence of freedom. It is also the essence of editing. Editors are scribes liberated to not simply record and disseminate information, but think hard about it, interpret, and ultimately, influence it.

The greatest challenge for editors has always been just how far to influence a writer's work. At what point does aid turn into meddling and, worse, betrayal? With dead writers, editors have had a long leash. With the living, editors have needed to learn to relinquish control. As centuries have unfurled, the best editors have learned to balance editorial queries with a writer's interests.

Like the best professional editors, self-editors need to balance the writer and reader roles. The reader and writer inside us vie for power yet, ideally, remain equal. In American society, though, we are led to see our reader-half as pedestrian, secondary, servile; and our writer-half as primary, precious, and ingenious. We are not generally taught the glory and creativity of reading, but the utility of it. By defining successful writers as celebrities, for instance, our media, publishing industry, and educational system train us to view readers, in contrast, as nerds, and reading as functional—a service we offer up to the author, who appears to cook up a book by putting his brilliance in a pot and stirring. We are rarely told that it is the nerdy reader in every serious writer that makes the ultimate creative decisions.

The more we view writers as icons, the more we unduly belittle the reader's power. When, for example, at the age of eighty, Günter Grass, the distinguished author and critic of fascism, admitted he had joined the Waffen SS at seventeen, most Germans, and many non-Germans, were outraged and went so far as to retract their love for his books. Yet Grass's moral debacle, as well as his formerly sterling reputation, are irrelevant to our reading of his writing. Nothing can change or dictate our experience of reading *The Tin Drum*, not even disillusionment with its author.

Reading, at bottom, has very little to do with writers. The celebrity author is a farce, because writing can only mean something once the author has removed himself from it. As Manguel puts it,

> in order for a text to be finished the writer must withdraw, cease to exist. While the writer remains present, the text remains incomplete. . . . Only when the able eye makes contact with the markings on the tablet, does the text come to active life. All writing depends on the generosity of the reader. . . . From its very start, reading is writing's apotheosis.

Writers stop writing a text at some point, with the knowledge that something, if only a word, might still, might always be changed for the better. Readers, not the writer, then finish the work, again and again, with their interpretations of it. When we honor a reader's true impact on writing, we begin to understand how to edit ourselves well. To make a work come close to what we want it to be, we have to finish writing as a reader.

╌╌

In the short history that follows, we will see how reading can hurt as well as save writing. Editors have evolved over the centuries from constricted to authoritative to collaborative, with variations in between. They have been helpful and destructive by turns, and on occasion, simultaneously. Ego and fear in an editor have mangled writing, whereas other texts have been enhanced by an editor's sensitivity, erudition, and sense of adventure.

May this chapter encourage us to purge ego and fear when we edit ourselves, and to cultivate our sensitivity, erudition, and sense of adventure.

TENTATIVE BEGINNINGS

In ancient times, scribes were obliged to take dictation and recite, but, as noted, refrain from really reading the words they wrote. With the medieval era approaching, they began to liberate their inner-reader. Medieval monks copied religious texts with the diligence of Xerox machines, but fatigue and ambition corrupted their output. The sleepy scribe would accidentally skip or alter words; the arrogant yet lucid would rewrite an obtuse passage; the zealous would interpolate. Scribes had begun to mess with the message—by accident or will—and, in so doing, take the first step toward interpretive freedom. They affected text now, and no longer just relayed it.

Then came the great and irreversible leap. Printing was

invented in Germany in the late fifteenth century to replace magnificent, but painstaking, script. And the stylus-wielding scribe, guilty for his opinions, metamorphosed into an editor who traded in them.

EDITORS OF POWER AND RENOWN

The sixteenth century gave editors more prominence than they'd ever had or would have again in the history of editing. With the celebrated authors of the day (Dante, Boccaccio, and Petrarch) having died over two centuries earlier, editors supplanted writers as the creative literary figures of the day.

In the absence of writers, readers and reading took center stage. In the 1500s, unlike today, reading was understood as an activity you did, not fast, but with varying levels of quality—an editor read well, okay, or poorly. Book buyers cared, in other words, how sensitive, frank, penetrating, and selective an editor was when he read. The quality of an editor's reading and how well he packaged a book had as much importance as how the book was written. Editors had "increasing prominence as individuals," writes Brian Richardson in *Print Culture in Renaissance Italy*, "each with his own distinctive approach to the shaping of a publication." In the clearest sign of this, the public sought out an editor's name on a book, not simply an author's.

It was an electric period of literary industry, and Venice, publishing's hub, brimmed with entrepreneurial drive and talent. Guiding this new world of print were the original freelance editors. Among them were Franciscan monks, teachers, law students, and writers. In a few short decades, the book industry was so successful that freelancers could live by editing alone. They helped publishers do several difficult jobs. Editors first had to locate and authenticate old manuscripts. Then they had to correct grammar, which, at the time, was a highly complicated task, since the Italian language was still forming itself. Once editors had decided a work was worthy of print and had copyedited it, they oiled its entry into the world with an exegesis—today's flap copy or scholarly introduction. These first industry editors created a tacit manifesto that still guides many editors today: be savvy enough to find good manuscripts, suave enough to navigate their ambiguities, and erudite enough to discuss them persuasively.

The grammar battles of the period demonstrate how linguistic erudition and the editors who wielded it carried real power in society. With Italian vernacular an inchoate mixture of Latin and regional dialects, editorial disagreements abounded about spelling, syntactical style, and a newly invented system of punctuation. Dialects were doing ferocious battle to become the single national language. Florence and Venice sparred for national prominence, and editors held the politically loaded role of deciding which flag the Italian vernacular would fly. In the poem *Italia mia* by Petrarch, for instance, editor Pietro Bembo restored the Tuscan spelling of "bavarico" and rejected "barbarico." He found "bavarico" more elegant. Merely by choosing a Tuscan *v* over a Venetian *b* for one of Italy's most celebrated poets, Bembo helped shape standard Italian language and therefore the identity of his nation.

Among Renaissance editors, the big debate was how much to homogenize a text. Editors had to decide whether to water down classical Latin into pedestrian speech, so it would be understood by a general, uneducated public, or render it into a more sophisticated vernacular. Should an editor talk down to an audience— and offer facile pleasure—or press an audience to educate themselves? To spoon-feed or challenge readers, that was the question, and remains an important one in our era. Editor Francesco Robertello, taking an unusually honest and generous tack, did both: he made significant alterations, but published his conjectures, so the reader would know exactly how and how much he had altered a text. The edit became a tutorial.

Uneducated printers and copiers stirred the debate by changing the words of a text on a whim. Richardson reports that Florentine editor Vincenzio Borghini cautioned, in words that still resonate today: "Editors should beware of the tendency of scribes and printers to substitute rare words with a *lectio facilior*. . . . For editors, a little knowledge was a dangerous thing: they should be either ignorant, in which case they would not interfere with the text, or well informed, so that any changes were justified."

By 1546, warnings against editorial abuses could sound bitter. Take, for instance, Francesco Doni's: "one editor corrects in one way and another otherwise, some delete, some insert, some flay [the text] and others damage its hide. . . . [Beware] stubborn editors, because they don't follow what is written but carry on in their own way." Then, as now, depending on his scholarship, worldliness, humility, alertness, and delicacy of ear, an editor respected or diluted a piece of writing.

By the end of the 1530s, works by living authors were getting published, and for the first time, editors had to figure out how to treat writers not only writing. The inevitable question of control arose. Who controlled a book—the person who wrote it or the one who made it possible for people to carry it around and read it at their leisure? In a situation that continues to this day, the editor held the writer hostage to his desire to reach a lot of readers. Against logic, it somehow became easy to think that a writer needed an editor more than the other way around.

The exchange between editors and writers in the early days of publishing appears to have been cooperative, but writers were not in control. Editors tended to dictate rather than collaborate. According to Richardson, Giorgio Vasari, author of *The Lives of the Artists*, was advised in 1550 to hire an editor and, in a bout of optimism, took on four. He requested they standardize his spelling but leave his style alone. Someone, however, ventured beyond turning his *t*s into *z*s, and tried to upgrade his original clumsy phrase "other temperas which time made them disappear" with "other temperas which, in the course of time, time made them disappear." Sometimes the medicine is worse than the disease. In a second edition, in 1568, the phrase was improved: "which in the course of time faded." The writer, though, had no say in all this. Because of deadline pressures, overextended publishers did what few would try today: they often skipped showing writers their final galley proofs.

COMMERCIAL MOTIVES

Renaissance editors worked, in the main, for companies, no longer oligarchs, and had a stake in their employer's success: if the company went under, the editor would lose his job. So despite their inclination as men of letters, editors now had commercial, not just literary, motives. "If a printer was to be more successful than his competitors," Richardson says, "then careful thought had to be given to the needs and expectations of a varied and widespread public." Accessible books naturally brought in more money than difficult ones. If contemporary publishing caters too much to the masses, it did not invent the practice. Four hundred years ago, editors were altering texts to make them easier for people to read. Sometimes their alterations were sensitive adaptations that allowed laypeople the pleasure of reading a classic; other times, editing obliterated the original.

How editors and living writers worked together from the late sixteenth to the mid-nineteenth century is, for the most part, woefully undocumented. The Catholic Church held strict rule over art for most of that time, and a suite of prudish popes and draconian Councils turned editing largely into censorship. Publishers and editors were preoccupied with trying to stay out of jail.

In the nineteenth century, the enduring business, with a capital B, of literature was faithfully depicted in George Gissing's novel *New Grub Street*. In his ruthless portrait of Victorian publishing in London, an editor's main role was to increase profits. The character Jasper Milvain, a journalist and aspiring editor, compared himself to his novelist friend Reardon and found his friend lacking. Reardon was incapable of being practical. He wrote to the order of his muse and could not bring himself to edit the few precious words he managed to eek out each week:

> He is the old type of unpractical artist; I am the literary man of 1882. He won't make concessions, or rather, he can't make them; he can't supply the market. . . . Literature nowadays is a trade. Putting aside men of genius, who may succeed by mere cosmic force, your successful man of letters is your skilful tradesman. He thinks first and foremost

of the markets; when one kind of goods begins to go off slackly, he is ready with something new and appetizing.

The purist artiste refused to have his work bowdlerized and suffered financially (Reardon), whereas the "player" who edited his work or allowed it to be edited to please the public reaped fame and fortune. Milvain's pandering self-editing is a warning against the temptation to please others and, in the process, lose our dignity as writers. But the novel does justice to the truly complicated nature of editing. Milvain respects editing, but misuses it. Reardon scorns editing, but really needs it. Reardon's writing is indulgent, not just pure; the reader's respect for the "real" writer's dignity is mixed with disappointment in his lack of discipline.

EDITORS AS CENSORS AND USURPERS

The white-knuckled grip of censorship slackened in the late nineteenth and early twentieth centuries, but laws differed from country to country. Censorship would continue in fits and starts with the banning of works in America by such luminaries as James Joyce, Aldous Huxley, and Ernest Hemingway. For the most part, though, in Europe and the United States strict governmental monitoring abated as modern times advanced.

But by the time various laws were relaxed in the 1800s, the English, French, and Americans, in their very different ways, had become automatic about censoring. Editors kept a censorship mentality even after they were legally free to relax it. Fearful editors would immunize themselves from prosecution by plucking out what they considered potentially offensive phrases.

American and English writers needed a thick skin against the knife of paranoid magazine editors. Thomas Hardy, Charles

Dickens, Mark Twain, and others were heavily edited with puritanical hands. Hardy's words were daintified, for instance, for *Far from the Madding Crowd*: "lewd" became "gross," "loose" became "wicked," "bawdy" became "sinful." Emily Dickinson, too, ran into an editor's squeamishness. Her poem "I taste a liquor never brewed" was first printed in 1861 in the *Springfield Daily Republican*. In that paper, the first stanza read:

> *I taste a liquor never brewed,*
> *From tankards scooped in pearl;*
> *Not Frankfort berries yield the sense*
> *Such a delirious whirl.*

These, however, were not Dickinson's words. Her stanza was more brazen and forthright. It carefully omitted a beat in the third line, which braced the reader for the fourth, where there was no facile rhyme (pearl/whirl) or anodyne phrase (a delirious whirl). Here is the real McCoy:

> *I taste a liquor never brewed—*
> *From Tankards scooped in Pearl—*
> *Not all the Frankfort Berries*
> *Yield such an Alcohol!*

With only a few extra words and a switch to common punctuation, the editor made the poem more ladylike and acceptable to a mass public. Dickinson wondered, understandably, "how one can publish and at the same time preserve the integrity of one's art?"

In the first decades of the twentieth century, when America

was convulsing from modernist rebellions against Victorian decorum, editors were a largely conservative lot tethered to old polite customs. To their writers' dismay, they deleted controversial words or scenes to please a priggish press and public. In 1929, even Max Perkins, despite his disgust for censorship, partook. "If," he argued to Ernest Hemingway about *A Farewell to Arms*, "we can bring out this serial [in *Scribner's Magazine*] without arousing too serious objection, you will have enormously consolidated your position, and will henceforth be further beyond objectionable criticism of a kind which is very bad because it prevents so many people from looking at the thing itself on its merits." Perkins's uncharacteristically strained plea ignored what he and his author both knew: fiddling with a word here or there was no light matter. Hemingway protested Perkins's plan to remove vulgarity from the text but, in the end, yielded.

It is bad enough for an editor to prune provocative phrases or ideas from a writer's work out of fear they will offend; when writers do this to themselves, one might wonder why they write at all.

AN EARLY EDITORIAL COLLABORATION: MARRIED AND FRAUGHT

One French writer, with the help of her editor, would triumph over censorship by writing sensualist novels without apology: Colette. For Colette, the fruits of editing were bittersweet, and included wise counsel and betrayal, intimacy and degradation.

Colette's editor was her husband, Willy, born Henri Gauthier-Villars. Willy was a writer, editor, and impresario who ran a ghost-writing factory, where he hired writers to make books from his ideas, which he would edit. Colette both benefited and suffered from Willy's industrial view of editing. She was a protégée of his seasoned methods for creating a compelling narrative. Yet even as his editing enhanced her talent, his commercialism warped it.

Their editing relationship began with Colette's first novel, *Claudine at School*. Willy had read it in draft and deemed it worthless, then, a few years later, reread it and changed his mind. In 1900, once a publisher had been secured, Willy edited the book with, Colette later recalled, "urgent and precise suggestions." This was the first of many collaborative books to follow.

The nature of their collaboration—how much Willy edited or wrote—has long been a juicy topic of belles lettres discourse. Judith Thurman, in her formidable biography of Colette, *Secrets of the Flesh*, writes, "There is no serious question about the true authorship of the *Claudines*. Colette wrote them, and they are in every sense, including morally, her intellectual property. Willy edited them; helped to shape them, influenced their tone."

One might wonder, for better or worse? Thurman concludes,

> Colette . . . claims that Willy's contributions vulgarized her work, but a careful reading reveals that they sometimes refined it. . . . [Willy] was a seasoned writer and editor who took her first manuscript in hand. It is apparent . . . that he helped her develop the characters both on and off the page; that he fine-tuned her prose; that he supplied references and opinions; that he added words, sentences, even passages.

The lessons of self-editing can come from unexpected sources; even a belligerent and uncouth editor might make a fine contribution to a book and to a writer's education. Willy taught Colette much about how to edit herself, but did so with all the delicacy

and deference of a vaudeville producer. Years later, Colette imper-
sonated his editing style to an interviewer: "You couldn't . . . warm
this up a bit? . . . For example, between Claudine and one of her
girlfriends, an overly close friendship . . . (he used another briefer
expression to make himself understood). And then some rural
slang, lots of rural slang. . . . Some girlish high jinx. . . . You see
what I mean?" Willy's crass commandeering alienated Colette.
She would eventually refuse his suggestions—both because their
personal relations had deteriorated and her prowess had matured.

It would be a mistake to think Colette's final, fiery rejection
of Willy's editing was the fallout from a failed marriage alone. As
so many writers do, she had invested a lot in her editor, who, to
complicate matters, happened to also be her husband. It is not
uncommon that writers—from Colette to Thomas Wolfe to
Raymond Carver—grow up, personally and artistically, only to
jettison the editor who helped them to maturity. The parental
aspect of editing cannot be overstated. Editing mentorships can
become stifling, and, to tinker with Freud's Oedipal theory, writers have to kill their parent to become mature writers (and self-
editors) themselves.

EDITING AS COLLABORATION: THE GOLDEN PERIOD

As the twentieth century took wing, editing acquired a new
creativity and grace. To listen hard to a writer and work *with*,
rather than *on*, him was a modern concept.

Max Perkins, an editor at Charles Scribner's Sons, whose writers included Hemingway, F. Scott Fitzgerald, and Thomas Wolfe,
epitomized the modern ideal of collaboration, where an editor
would engage energetically, but never invasively, in a writer's

work. As one of his writers, Mozart biographer Marcia Davenport, put it, Perkins's "essential quality was always to say little, but by powerful empathy for writers and for books to draw out of them what they had it in them to say and to write." Alice (Roosevelt) Longworth was a good example. Perkins agreed to publish a memoir of her saucy life as the president's daughter and Washington socialite. But like many people, Longworth was better in conversation than on paper. In her writing, she told trivial things that didn't matter and held back those that did. Perkins read her first batch of reminiscences and wrote to a friend, "I was really cold with panic." The panicked editor did the only thing he knew to do. He set to work. Perkins studied Longworth's every sentence with her. He gave her ongoing advice, including to slow down and "make every person a character and make every action an event." In *Max Perkins: Editor of Genius*, A. Scott Berg writes, "As [Longworth] wrote she imagined Perkins standing over her shoulder, asking her questions. Within five or six months, Mrs. Longworth's writing had improved. . . . What began as a bloodless work of disconnected memories took on definition and shape and even got somewhat tart." Perkins told the friend to whom he'd earlier confessed panic, "we made a silk purse out of a sow's ear with Alice Longworth's book—or she did." She did it, with his indispensable help; yet, Perkins taught her a way to edit that she could keep and use again without him. With Longworth, he achieved what can be one of an editor's most satisfying tasks: to teach writers to self-edit.

There were others in Perkins's time who edited with gumption, such as Horace Liveright, whose firm Boni & Liveright published Ezra Pound, T. S. Eliot, and Djuna Barnes. Liveright spearheaded the loud, inventive marketing of fine and unconventional literature. Editors Eugene Saxton and Elizabeth Lawrence at Harper & Brothers, who worked with Betty Smith on *A Tree Grows in Brooklyn*, were also highly regarded. But for getting deep in the trenches with writer after writer, Perkins was the man. It was as if editing had to keep pace with breakthroughs in arts and letters, and Perkins saw this. Alongside Marcel Duchamp and Picasso in the visual arts, writers such as Hemingway, Gertrude Stein, Ford Madox Ford, James Baldwin, and Fitzgerald revolutionized the literary vernacular. Editors had to listen very hard now to understand and help a writer—harder than in centuries past, when most unconventional writers still followed certain rhetorical codes. Now the codes themselves were being reworked or shunned. Perkins responded to the elasticity of modern prose by rejecting editorial rigidity and becoming elastic himself.

THE WRITER AS EDITOR

Although Perkins was the first at Scribner's to edit so deeply, Ezra Pound had already edited to the bone in 1921. Pound, the renowned poet, magazine editor, and literary liaison, edited *The Waste Land*, for which, years later, T. S. Eliot would pay him tribute: "He was a marvelous critic because he didn't try to turn you into an imitation of himself. He tried to see what you were trying to do."

But according to scholar Donald Gallup, Pound was not as open-minded as Eliot says. For one thing, Eliot loved theater and wanted to use theatrical elements in his poem; Pound ruled theater out for his protégé, calling it didactic, "bad," and unsuited to poetry. A second interdiction arose when Eliot wanted to use prose as a transitional link for verse. Pound protested that prosaic interludes weakened a poem's intensity. While another editor might have overlooked his differences with a writer to help improve what the writer set out to do, Pound rejected Eliot's ideas outright. "Pound's major deletions in the central poem," writes Gallup,

> . . . reflect a lack of sympathy with some of the experiments that Eliot was trying to carry out. The poem which resulted from the Eliot-Pound collaboration was in some respects quite different from that which Eliot had had in mind. At least part of what the central poem gained in concentration, intensity, and general effectiveness through Pound's editing was at the sacrifice of some of its experimental character.

It is impossible to know if Eliot's poem could have succeeded with both "concentration" and a more "experimental character." Eliot did approve Pound's edit. It is hard, though, not to wonder what *The Waste Land* would have been like if its author had edited it more independently.

Is it possible that Pound's luminous personality blinded Eliot? Unlike the self-effacing Perkins, Pound spoke with the boom and lilt of a Shakespearean actor, and had stone-strong opinions. Eliot was, at the time, periodically sick, poor, and struggling to find his way with his work—artistically and financially. It is easy to imagine that a writer unmoored will grab on to his editor's views, as a tired swimmer to a raft. When we edit, we should take care not to overpower a writer who may be vulnerable. And if we are that writer, we should beware domineering editors who, without malice, may mislead.

Despite his authoritarianism, Pound was, Gallup concedes, an editorial genius: with *The Waste Land* he cleared away the brush and helped recycle poetic debris into the central poem. Himself a writer above all else, Pound was no doubt extra finely attuned as an editor. "Certainly there is no more useful criticism and no more precious praise for a poet," writes Eliot, "than that of another poet." To further the point, he says, "I wished . . . to honour the technical mastery and critical ability manifest in [Pound's] . . . own work, which had also done so much to turn *The Waste Land* from a jumble of good and bad passages into a poem."

It would be easy to believe that writers best understand the mechanics of writing and therefore make the best editors. Many writers do make superb editors. But then again, many do not. Many do not have the patience to investigate another writer's work—they would always rather be investigating their own. Or they see another's words through the lens of how they themselves would write them. Pound appears, at times, for instance, to have edited *The Waste Land* as if he were writing it. Or take Edith Wharton, who in her response to *The Great Gatsby* wished that Fitzgerald had "given us [Gatsby's] early career . . . instead of a short resumé of it. That would have situated him, & made his final tragedy a tragedy instead of a 'fait divers' for the morning papers." Wharton would have edited Fitzgerald's novel, in other words, so that it came out sounding like her own.

HOUSE STYLE: *THE NEW YORKER*

There are and always have been great editors who are naturally sensitive to writing and writers, without being writers themselves. Perkins, who limited himself to eloquent missives, is a prime example. Several others worked at *The New Yorker*.

The New Yorker was, from its inception in 1924, renowned for its zealous editorial approach. In Ben Yagoda's chronicle *About Town*, the current *New Yorker*'s famously strict editing can be traced back to founder Harold Ross's "notorious insistence that the circumstantial elements of a piece, fact or fiction, be identified or 'pegged' in the first one or two paragraphs." *The New Yorker* wanted a story—fictional or factual—to be immediately clear, at the start and throughout. Ross's editorial protégés, such as Katharine Angell (later White), E. B. White, and William Shawn, would, with occasional resistance from writers, carry out Ross's dictum to render writing smooth and genial for the reader.

Nabokov was a persuasive resister. In the 1940s, he wrote a series of rebukes to the Rossian edit. The first, to Edmund Wilson, dealt with his story "Double Talk": "A man called Ross started to 'edit' it, and I wrote to Mrs. White telling her that I could not accept any of those ridiculous and exasperating alterations (odds and ends inserted in order to 'link up' ideas and make them clear to the 'average reader')."

Since the point was to be straightforward at all costs, "overwriting" and unconventional syntax were outlawed at the magazine. When White took over editing Nabokov, she had the good sense to adjust the rules for him. He wrote her more of his thoughts on editing:

> I deeply appreciated your sympathetic handling of "My Uncle." It is the principle itself of editing that distresses me. I should be very grateful to you if you help me to weed out bad grammar but I do not think I would like my longish sentences clipped too close, or those drawbridges lowered which I have taken such pains to lift. In other words, I would like to discriminate between awkward con-

struction (which is bad) and a certain special—how shall I put it—sinuosity, which is my own and which only at first glance may seem awkward or obscure. Why not have the reader re-read a sentence now and then? It won't hurt him.

White, to her credit, evolved as an editor to meet her writer's demands. Two years later, Nabokov sent her "Lance," a futuristic, layered story whose style was antithetical to the magazine's. White took it anyway, and harking back to Renaissance editors, sent readers a one-paragraph exegesis to help them understand the story (which Nabokov applauded—it must have seemed preferable to having his prose disfigured). Another two years later, editor and writer had gone a distance together. Nabokov praised White—not without a tincture of irony—for her substantial edit of a chapter from *Pnin*: "You have done a magnificent job. While reading your script I felt like a patient reclining under the glitter of delicate instruments. I am still under the spell of your novocaine and hastily return these pages before I start aching."

With Nabokov, *The New Yorker* broke its own rules for the sake of something grand. Self-editors should take note, and similarly break their own editing rules or patterns to create something fresh.

When William Shawn replaced Ross in 1952, he turned up the volume on the magazine's grammatical finickiness. In Yagoda's account, Shawn's greatest weakness was his quest for perfection where none was possible. Ironically, his fetishization of grammar turned *New Yorker* sentences inside out, from, at their worst, short and dull, to mazelike collections of "which"s and "that"s and commas; what Tom Wolfe satirized as "whichy thickets." The point was still clarity, but now the route there was to say everything, and leave no clause unturned. The result was a caricature of "correct" writing, as found in Shawn's bible, Fowler's *Modern English Usage*.

One unfortunate result of both the Ross and Shawn reigns was that some writers, as Yagoda puts it, "internalized the magazine's approach and saw their prose lose liveliness, individuality, and grace as a result." Kenneth Tynan, for instance, worried that *New Yorker* editing removed "much that might have made [my piece] identifiably mine; also, when writing for the magazine, one automatically censors audacious phrases lest they should be demolished by the inquisitorial logicians on 43rd St." He referred to the queries the editor made on his proofs as "an artillery bombardment." For some writers, Shawn's approach felt like censorship. His inflexibility frightened their truest voice into hiding. The self-censorship Tynan describes mocks the very idea of a writer's voice. When writing is an art as much as a tool for transmitting information, the writer cannot edit himself with an editor's—or anyone's—systematic disapproval in mind. Auden's Inner Censorate, discussed in chapter one, can be an effective insurance policy against indulgence. But we must not pervert the Inner Censorate into an internalized linguistic police.

For certain writers, though, Shawn was a saint. He had one quality that every editor should have, but too many do not: Shawn knew how to listen to and trust writers through all the fumbling stages of their writing process. Some of America's finest authors worshipped him for this. J. D. Salinger dedicated his book *Franny and Zooey* to "my editor, mentor and (heaven help him) closest friend, William Shawn, *genius domus* of *The New Yorker*, lover of the long shot, protector of the unprolific, defender of the hopelessly flamboyant, most unreasonably modest of born great artist-editors." Salinger understood that an editor's job goes far beyond grammarian and taste arbiter, and includes setting a tone for a writer's working life. An editor might, with attentiveness, compassion, and insight, secure a writer emotionally enough to free him artistically.

Shawn helped the writer John Cheever feel no less than "alive." In a letter to Shawn's wife, Emmy, Cheever wrote,

> As for [*The Wapshot Chronicle*] I sometimes wonder if Bill knows how important he was. One always writes for someone and much of it was written for Bill. The advice he gave me and the advice he didn't give me was all brilliant and he wired when he read it which makes the difference between feeling alive and feeling like an old suit hanging in a closet.

Shawn tended his authors as a gardener his plants—some were cacti, some orchids, but all got their requisite water. An editor's attention goes a long way to soothe and motivate a writer, whose life can, in periods, smack of solitary confinement.

With his superhuman patience and focus that made writers believe their ideas, and, by extension, they themselves, were important, Shawn was the Perkins of his time. Writer Ved Mehta gives the most vivid description of what made Shawn a "great artist-editor":

> I had never before had anyone in my life listen to me at as deep a level as he was doing, with no wish to judge— with only boundless interest and curiosity. . . . Most people in conversation tried to impress you, hurried you along, had their own preconceptions or agendas, or were dis-

tracted by their own worries or cares. In contrast, he seemed to absorb words as a musician absorbs music.

To *listen* well—this was Shawn's gift and the high bar every editor, and self-editor, must try to reach.

AN EDITING COLLABORATION
IN THE CORPORATE WORLD

Shawn left *The New Yorker* in 1987. Since then, artist-editors have not, contrary to general opinion, gone extinct. In today's era of corporate-led expedience, there are some editors who remain conscientious and creative.

The following account of how Robin Robertson, editorial director of Jonathan Cape in London, edited Adam Thorpe's novel *Ulverton* (told to me through interviews), brings this brief history into our times; and demonstrates that since the epoch of scribes, editing has become, at its best, a creative and sophisticated act—if publishers would only allow editors enough time to perform it. Most do not. The following account provides a final portrait of first-rate editing, but most importantly, it is a final, rich lesson for editing ourselves.

Robertson's editorial approach, for instance, easily translates into a method for self-editing: *First pass*, he reads the entire text, with as few interruptions as possible—"as a reader would." He prefers not to read a book partially, "as the editor's eye should not—ideally—pass over the text too many times, for fear of losing the very objectivity the writer lacks." At this point, he says, he is "looking for the general shape: the rhythm, the consistency of the prose—feeling for slackening of tension, extraneous scenes or characters, narrative lacunae, etc.—and watching myself for the first signs of inattention which may be occasioned by a turgidity or imprecision in the prose." Robertson will discuss his findings with the author, hoping that, "through this conversation, we both might close in on the faults. The crucial thing is to encourage the writer to see the problem himself, as he is the one best able to correct it."

Robertson will ask the writer to iron out the "larger structural flaws, extravagances and longeurs." Once that's done, he'll make a *second pass*. At this stage, he presumes "that the car has a chassis, four wheels and a working engine, but may still benefit from tuning, lubrication and a paint job—and, if required, some optional extras." In the *third pass*, he says, "macro cedes to micro."

A successful self-edit involves each step that Robertson describes, and hinges on self-surveillance: watching ourselves "for the first signs of inattention," watching ourselves read.

⌒

In 1991, Robertson bought and edited Thorpe's first novel, *Ulverton*, which would become a Booker Prize nominee that critic Richard Eder would call "almost literally transporting."

The novel tells the history of a fictional English village, from 1650 to 1988, through a series of self-contained but discreetly interlocking stories a generation or two apart. The book is about the land itself as much as the lives lived on and buried in it. Each chapter presents a different first-person narrative source. There are, for example, a farmer's diary (1712), letters by a noblewoman to her lover (1743), and a television documentary (1988). The result is a novelistic patchwork, with the thread of lineage connecting one end to the other.

The novel's dialogue brings to life, among others, a busybody shepherd, a gentleman farmer obsessed by new science, and a developer inadvertently digging up the town's bones. In the 1712 farmer's log, for example, we read, "The maid has taken to a fuller skirt. She appears robust. I have put aside already the cost of her carrying, which she agreed at 7s, which is indeed a princely sum for a natural task, involving as it did her pleasure, which I have asked the Lord His forgiveness for."

The *Ulverton* edit began when Thorpe sent Robertson individual chapters as he finished them. Though Robertson prefers not to read a manuscript partially, he agreed to read these chapters in isolation, for later, read together with their historical linkages, they would create a different effect. No actual editing was done, though, until the manuscript was finished. "Being edited at the end of the process was right," Thorpe says. "Working on the chapters before the whole was finished would have caused me to stumble, get distracted."

Once he had the entire manuscript, Robertson told Thorpe where he saw problems—mainly excesses and obscurities. Thorpe revised. The edit intensified when Robertson spent a few days at the writer's home in southern France "tying up loose ends." The visit was critical to the novel's development. Spending days together allowed editor and writer to go further with the book's details than if they'd edited entirely by phone. Thorpe recalls:

> Robin read through two reworked chapters while lying prone in the garden because of a bad back, amid the shrills of cicadas. I looked down nervously from the study window— one of the chapters was the Molly Bloom–like monologue of the labourer, Jo Perry, written in broad dialect. (It was

entirely rewritten after both Robin and my agent found the original too long and dull.) "It's great," he said, emerging from the hot sunlight. "Much better. Very strong." Nothing, to my relief and astonishment, on its difficulty. "Could you read it OK?" I asked. "Sure. It'll lose you some support, and annoy the critics, but that's good." It had integrity, we agreed. That chapter probably screwed the commercial success of the novel, but integrity is worth so much more, and Robin recognizes that.

Your editor need not come into your home, share your food, and lie in your garden. This kind of bond is, for a variety of reasons, not always possible or appropriate. The risks of getting too close are many: the writer may lean too hard on his editor, ask for money, call at midnight with private woes; or the editor may become intrusive, read the writer's work as if it were his palm. There are, nonetheless, benefits to editing outside the usually officious and overworked atmosphere of an editor's office. "Staying with us," Thorpe says, "Robin could focus more clearly and relaxedly on the work in hand." If all goes well, out of intimacy comes trust; and trust is the foundation of a good edit.

On his own, Thorpe tried to keep track of his multigenerational view of one large tract of land. He drew a fictional map of the village that he kept on his wall as he wrote. "It didn't help my imaginative grasp of the place," he says, "but it prevented confusion." Complication, though, if not confusion, abounded. Robertson's edit aimed straight at *Ulverton*'s complexities:

On account of the multi-layered, interwoven nature of the book there was always the risk that some of the strands might slip from view, that others might overpower, or that the desired connections might not be made. . . . I saw quite early on that the novel had to be edited like a poem, as each story and character and image had ramifications and concatenations; that everything connected; that nothing was there by accident. So, my job was to monitor the free-flow and encourage the connotative, but avoid any false or lost trails and guard against any sense of the inorganic or architectonic.

Adam made it very easy for me because he knew exactly what he was doing. I had a lot of regressive fun with colour-coded motif charts, but the car was almost ready; I just supplied the go-faster stripes.

Thorpe and Robertson put the text under an imaginary loupe to magnify the minuscule. They invented devices to track the book's countless symbolic details. Robertson, for instance, drew an intricate chart of leitmotivs (e.g., red ribbon, bedwine, angel, shepherds' ghost), and together they filled it in across the chapters. Where there were gaps, Thorpe inserted the leitmotiv, subtly weaving it into the story, he says, "to get a more even spread or livelier current."

Red ribbons, and ribbonlike bandages, for instance, work a symbolic spell throughout the text. They act, the author says, "as displaced erotic passion."

The ribbons prompted me, in each story, to show a hopeless passion. . . . I went back to the first story and had Gabby pull out the ribbons from his tunic—adding his speech about Anne wanting her hair to be "all up in silks."

. . . It is for me one of the most important moments in the first chapter, and is seminal to the theme of "hopeless hoping" in the novel. . . . Yet it wasn't there in the first draft written some years before.

Thorpe describes this process of sharpening the book's symbols as "refining the leit-motif table," recalling the green light Fitzgerald added to the beginning of *The Great Gatsby* after Perkins's edit. Thorpe nevertheless took care to let his symbolism breathe: "I had to resist too tight a weave of continuity, too easy a symbolic, literary continuum. The readers had to feel that they were discovering links for themselves, creatively. There are links that have grown organically since, that I didn't intend." Thorpe's generous discussion of the symbolism in *Ulverton* adds a great deal to our understanding of leitmotiv.

For Robertson, an editorial conversation with a writer should trade on "sensitivity, patience, doubt and certainty." Arrogance can have no part. The same qualities are essential to the conversation we have with ourselves when we edit. For Robertson,

the easiest aspect of editing is either working with a writer who knows precisely what he's up to, like Adam, or with one who doesn't have a clue but is receptive. The first requires the merest nudge; the second will allow you a breathtakingly free rein to re-write. . . .

The hardest aspect is when the author doesn't have an over-arching idea for the text, doesn't see when he is writing well or writing badly, and is not amenable to constructive suggestion.

The hardest aspect of editing is the hardest aspect of self-editing too. We can edit far on our own if we can find an over-arching idea for our work, see where we are writing well or badly, and stay amenable to trying something new.

In the best of situations, the current publish-for-profit culture makes it impossible for editors to always give everything that a writer wants. Despite Thorpe's long standing with Robertson, for instance (they've worked on ten books together), Thorpe says sometimes a book of his is "too large to edit properly—it would demand two weeks' mutual attention and this is now not possible (or at least not for my work) in the busy professional field." Thorpe implies what is well known: editors are given time to straighten out a blockbuster, but not always a literary novel destined for relatively modest sales. Like every writer I know, Thorpe recoils at the publishing monolith, of which Robertson is an undeniable part: "I have to be armoured to take on Robin's professional side, and not to feel winded by the idea that I'm just another name on his long list. He's part of the literary army, I'm alone."

The *Ulverton* edit was ideal, but circumstances change with every book. Thorpe knows that in the long run, he has to rely most on himself.

⌒

In the last thousand years, editors have roughly gone from servile to celebrated to censorial to collaborative, and finally, to corporate. The most superb editors in any era cannot always come through for a writer. They may be brilliant, but coercive, like Pound; patient, but autocratic, like Shawn; or well intentioned, but squeezed for time, like most editors working today. Therefore, we must read our own drafts with strict care and pride; the way we read, not just write, will matter immensely.

In our era, more than some others, writers must buck up and take care of themselves. And this isn't a bad thing. Veteran editor Gerald Howard has no patience for "the writer's idealization of the editor as his savior." The marvelous Max Perkins, he believes, corrupted generations of "naïve writers who feel that somehow if they can meet their Max Perkins, then they'll become Tom Wolfe." Howard rightly cries: "Become Tom Wolfe yourself!"

Susan Bell

One Doesn't Just Write a Book, One Makes a Book
Michael Ondaatje

The thing is you have to allow yourself to be as anarchic as possible about your own material, just so you're not protecting it too much. It could mean dropping the first fifty pages of a book or the last fifty pages, or beginning at the end. I try all kinds of, not tricks so much, but ways to accuse the text: Is this really valuable? When you go back you are stricter with the material. You see things more. Like what's important about this scene is this moment here and not the whole buildup to it; and you work those crucial ten lines in somewhere else. Often you can fix a scene at point M by redoing something at point F, which is a very interesting aspect of editing. If there's a problem at a certain point in the book, the way to fix it often is to do something somewhere else. Often the solution might be going back and finding something that I had and reworking that into the right place in the book. There's a slush pile of material there that I need to use.

⌣

I began as a poet. I had a teacher who was sort of my guru, and I gave him my manuscript of about thirty or forty poems. He looked at it and said, "Now you have to shape it. Now you have to make a book out of it. It's not just a collection of thirty or forty poems." So very early on I learned that apart from the content of a book, even of poems, one has to find a structure for it. Later, with Billy the Kid, *the shape of it was like a collage and I was conscious of how the poems were aligned to each other, how they jostled against each other. There was a kind of narrative line in the overall arc of the thing, but within that arc, you were involved with placement—where you placed the poem and which you placed it beside. This links up with design and how much white space there is and so forth. Just being aware of that element of structure was very important to me from the word go. I learned early on that one doesn't just write a book, one makes a book.*

Years ago, I saw a documentary on a New York artist, I can't remember who, and at one point in the last stages of completing the work, he had two assistants go and hold up pieces of wood to reframe the thing, to see how big it should be, should they close in the frame a little bit more, make the area smaller or leave the complete thing— and that fascinated me. I'm very, very conscious of the overall frame of the novel, and how you can take it in a few inches or a foot, like a painting, and change the overall shape and design and look of it, and theme of it, as a result.

I write the first draft of a novel in notebooks over a period of say two or three years, and then I spend about a couple of years editing them. I just keep going through it again and again and again. Each time, whatever doesn't interest me any more drops away. I keep adding, too, new stuff that interests me. So the first three years are spent trying to find the structure, find the story. There's a stage where you start compressing and pulling stuff away and adding stuff and realizing you're looking at the text not as someone who is inventing a story, but who's trying to shape a story.

I reread nothing. I intentionally don't look at the stuff at all until I've finished the book. At that stage when you go back and reread for the first time, it's kind of horrific. But I don't want to have everything perfectly made before I take the next step. It seems like moving forward with armed guards. There isn't an element of danger or risk or that anything possible can happen in the next scene. Having a concept of what the book is exactly about before you begin it is a tremendous limitation, because no idea is going to be as intricate and complicated as what you will discover in that process of writing it.

At some stage in the book, I'm very conscious of what almost every scene does, and I'll make it reflect the larger structure of the book, or fit into the larger structure, not just in a casual, accidental way. It may feel accidental, but it's there for a purpose.

There are things like italics, or who speaks when, or when to go from Italy to England or India, or from character to character, all that stuff is decided in the editing stage. There's no map that I make beforehand. There's a map later on.

⌒

I'm trying to see how much I could pack into the boat and make it not sink at the same time. If I'm getting bored, then the reader is going to get bored.

⌒

I always write the beginning at the end. It's the last thing I write because then I know what the book is about.

⌒

I keep going until I can't do anything more, then I give it to two or three friends to read. Then I mull over what they say and rewrite a bit and after I've done that, I send it to the publisher. I never feel the book is finished until that very last time I spend with an editor on the book.

Seeing if a character is working, that's what's mostly useful from the two or three readers you give your manuscript to for the first time. They'll say "What happened to so and so, he was really interesting, and then disappears halfway through." Or we'll have a discussion about a character not being fully evolved. I really focus on character. If I haven't defined a character enough, I might put in something else. I can add something about that person buying some sausages, which might reveal something about him. Perhaps he doesn't tip the guy.

I hand in my books after obsessive editing on my own part. Working with an editor used to be very, very tense for me. It's become easier because I hand in the book at a later stage than I did at one time.

BASIC COPYEDITING
SYMBOLS

Insert a word or letter	∧
Delete a word	___ ∘
Delete a letter	ŷ
Transpose	(tr) /
Begin new paragraph	(new ¶)
Eliminate a paragraph break	(run in)
Remove space	◡ /
Insert space	# /
Retain original and ignore	(stet) /
Insert comma	⌃
Insert period	⊙
Insert quote marks	⌄⌄

Basic Copyediting Symbols

Insert apostrophe	⌄
Insert hyphen	=
Insert em dash	$\frac{1}{m}$
Italicize	(ital)/
Delete italics	(rom)/
Capital letter(s)	(cap)/
Lowercase	(lc)/

BIBLIOGRAPHY

Amis, Martin. *The War Against Cliché: Essays and Reviews, 1971–2000.* New York: Miramax Books, 2001.

Auden, W. H. *A Certain World: A Commonplace Book.* New York: Viking, 1970. (Contains quote by Paul Valéry.)

———. *The Dyer's Hand and Other Essays.* New York: Vintage, 1989.

Benjamin, Walter. "Post No Bills: The Writer's Technique in Thirteen Theses." In *One-Way Street and Other Writings.* London: Verso, 1997.

Berg, A. Scott. *Max Perkins: Editor of Genius.* New York: Riverhead Books, 1997.

Berger, Maurice. *White Lies: Race and the Myths of Whiteness.* New York: Farrar, Straus and Giroux, 1999.

Blake, Nicholas. *The Beast Must Die.* New York: HarperCollins, 1985.

Brillat-Savarin, Jean Anthelme. *The Physiology of Taste.* New York: Counterpoint Press, 2000.

Brown, Trisha. *Trisha Brown: Dance and Art in Dialogue, 1961–2001.* Edited by Hendel Teicher. Andover, Mass.: Addison Gallery of American Art, Phillips Academy, 2002.

Burroway, Janet. *Writing Fiction: A Guide to Narrative Craft.* 5th ed. New York: Longman, 2000.

Butler, Samuel. The *Notebooks of Samuel Butler.* McLean, Va.: IndyPublish.com, 2003.

Cain, James M. *The Postman Always Rings Twice*. New York: Vintage, 1989.

Caponegro, Mary. *The Star Café*. New York: Scribner, 1990.

———. "The Father's Blessing." In *The Complexities of Intimacy*. Minneapolis, Minn.: Coffee House Press, 2001.

Chandler, Raymond. *Trouble Is My Business*. New York: Vintage, 1988.

Chekhov, Anton. "The Black Monk." In *The Duel and Other Stories*. Translated with an introduction by Ronald Wilks. New York: Penguin, 1984.

———. "The Wife." In *The Duel and Other Stories*. Translated with an introduction by Ronald Wilks. New York: Penguin, 1984.

Chilcott, Tim. *A Publisher and His Circle: The Life and Works of John Taylor, Keats's Publisher*. London: Routledge & Kegan Paul, 1972.

Christin, Anne-Marie, ed. *A History of Writing: From Hieroglyph to Multimedia*. Paris: Flammarion, 2002.

Colette. *Oeuvres Tome 1*. Paris: Gallimard, 1984.

———. *The Claudine Novels*. Translated by Antonia White. New York: Penguin, 1990.

Cunard, Nancy. *These Were the Hours: Memories of My Hours Press, Réanville and Paris 1928–1931*. Carbondale: Southern Illinois University Press, 1969.

D'Agata, John. "The Scream." In *The Lifespan of a Fact* (read aloud at the New School). New York: Farrar, Straus and Giroux, forthcoming.

Dardis, Tom. *Firebrand: The Life of Horace Liveright*. New York: Random House, 1995.

Delacroix, Eugene. *The Journal of Eugene Delacroix*. London: Phaidon, 1995.

Dickinson, Emily. "The May-Wine." *Springfield Daily Republican,* May 4, 1861.

Diderot, Denis. *Jacques le Fataliste et son maître*. Paris: Buisson, 1796.

Didion, Joan. "On Morality." In *Slouching Towards Bethlehem*. New York: Farrar, Straus and Giroux, 1990.

Eder, Richard. "Hearts of Darkness." *New York Times Book Review,* February 6, 2000.

Eliot, T. S. *The Waste Land: A Facsimile and Transcript of the Original Drafts Including the Annotations of Ezra Pound.* Edited and with an introduction by Valerie Eliot. New York: Harcourt, 1971.

Epstein, Mitch. *Vietnam: A Book of Changes.* New York: W. W. Norton, 1996.

———. *Family Business.* Göettingen: Steidl, 2003.

Erickson, Steve. "Guilty Pleasures and Lost Causes." *Black Clock* no. 4, 2005.

Faulkner, William. In *William Faulkner: Three Decades of Criticism.* Edited by Frederick John Hoffman and Olga W. Vickery. New York: Harcourt, 1963.

Fitzgerald, F. Scott. *The Great Gatsby.* New York: Scribner, 1953.

———. *The Letters of F. Scott Fitzgerald.* Edited by Andrew Turnbull. New York: Scribner, 1963.

———. *The Great Gatsby: A Facsimile of the Manuscript.* Edited with an introduction by Matthew J. Bruccoli. Washington, D.C.: Microcard Editions Books, 1973.

———. *Correspondence of F. Scott Fitzgerald.* Edited by Matthew J. Bruccoli and Margaret M. Duggan, with Susan Walker. New York: Random House, 1980.

———. *The Crack-Up.* Edited by Edmund Wilson. New York: New Directions, 1993.

———. *A Life in Letters.* Edited by Matthew J. Bruccoli, with the assistance of Judith S. Baughman. New York: Scribner, 1994.

———. *The Great Gatsby.* Cambridge Edition. Edited by Matthew J. Bruccoli. Cambridge: Cambridge University Press, 1999.

Flaubert, Gustave. *The Selected Letters of Gustave Flaubert.* Translated and edited with an introduction by Francis Steegmuller. New York: Farrar, Straus and Giroux, 1953.

Franzen, Jonathan. *The Corrections.* New York: Farrar, Straus and Giroux, 2001.

Freeman, Judith. *Red Water*. New York: Pantheon, 2002.

Gallup, Donald. *T. S. Eliot & Ezra Pound, Collaborators in Letters*. New Haven, Conn.: Henry W. Wenning/C. A. Stonehill, 1970.

Gissing, George. *New Grub Street*. McLean, Va.: IndyPublish.com, 2006.

Gottlieb, Eli. *The Boy Who Went Away*. New York: St. Martin's Press, 1997.

Gross, Gerald, ed. *Editors on Editing*. New York: Grosset & Dunlap, 1962.

Hall, Donald. "With Jane and Without: An Interview with Donald Hall," with Jeffrey S. Cramer. *The Massachusetts Review* vol. 39, issue 4, 1998/1999.

Hammett, Dashiell. *Red Harvest*. New York: Vintage, 1989.

Hardy, Thomas. *Far from the Madding Crowd*. New York: Penguin, 1994.

Hawkes, John. *Travesty*. New York: New Directions, 1976.

Hemingway, Ernest. *A Farewell to Arms*. New York: Scribner, 1995.

Howard, Gerald. "Mistah Perkins, He Dead." *The American Scholar* vol. 58, no. 3, 1989.

James, Henry. *The Spoils of Poynton*. New York: Penguin Classics, 1988.

Johnson, Samuel. *Johnson on Johnson*. Edited by John Wain. London: J. M. Dent & Sons, 1976.

Joyce, James. *Ulysses*. New York: Vintage, 1990.

Kaplan, David Michael. *Revision: A Creative Approach to Writing and Rewriting Fiction*. Cincinnati, Ohio: Story Press, 1997.

Kapuściński, Ryszard. *The Emperor*. New York: Vintage, 1989.

Kerouac, Jack. Interview by Ted Berrigan, *The Paris Review* no. 41, issue 43, 1968.

Kidder, Tracy. *The Soul of a New Machine*. New York: Avon, 1981.

King, Stephen. *On Writing: A Memoir of the Craft*. New York: Simon & Schuster, 2000.

Kundera, Milan. *The Art of the Novel*. Translated by Linda Asher. New York: Perennial Library, 1988.

Lauterbach, Ann. "How I Think about What I Write." *New American Writing* 14, 1996.

Lehan, Richard. *The Great Gatsby: The Limits of Wonder*. Boston: Twayne, 1995.

Lewis, Jim. *The King Is Dead*. New York: Knopf, 2003.

Lowry, Martin. *The World of Aldus Manutius: Business and Scholarship in Renaissance Venice*. Oxford: Blackwell, 1979.

Mailer, Norman. *The Spooky Art: Some Thoughts on Writing*. New York: Random House, 2003.

Manguel, Alberto. *A History of Reading*. New York: Penguin, 1996.

Martin, Agnes. *Writings/Schriften*. Berlin and New York: Cantz-DAP, 1992.

Mathews, Harry. *The Human Country: New and Collected Stories*. Chicago: Dalkey Archive Press, 2002.

Matisse, Henri. *Cahiers Henri Matisse*. Nice: Musée Matisse, 1986.

Maugham, Somerset. *The Summing Up*. New York: Penguin Classics, 1992.

McDermott, Alice. *That Night*. New York: Farrar, Straus and Giroux, 1987.

McDonough, Tom. *Light Years*. New York: Grove Press, 1987.

Mencken, H. L. "The Great Gatsby." *Baltimore Evening Sun*, May 2, 1925.

Mobilio, Albert. *Me with Animal Towering*. New York: Four Walls Eight Windows, 2002.

Morrow, Bradford. "Lush." In *The O. Henry Prize Stories 2003*. Edited by Laura Furman. New York: Anchor Books, 2003.

Murch, Walter. In *The Conversations: Walter Murch and the Art of Editing Film* by Michael Ondaatje. New York: Knopf, 2002.

Naipaul, V. S. *A Bend in the River*. New York: Vintage, 1980.

O'Brien, Flann. *The Third Policeman*. Chicago: Dalkey Archive Press, 1999.

O'Hara, John. The Rider College Lectures. In *"An Artist Is His Own Fault": John O'Hara on Writers and Writing*. Edited and with an introduction by Matthew J. Bruccoli. Carbondale: Southern Illinois University Press, 1977.

———. *Appointment in Samarra.* New York: Vintage, 1982.

Ondaatje, Michael. *Anil's Ghost.* New York: Knopf, 2000.

———. *The Conversations: Walter Murch and the Art of Editing Film.* New York: Knopf, 2002.

Pärt, Arvo. *Arvo Pärt: 24 Preludes for a Fugue.* DVD. Directed by Dorian Supin, 2004. Distributed by Naxos, 2005.

Patchett, Ann. *Truth and Beauty: A Friendship.* New York: Harper-Collins, 2004.

Perkins, Maxwell. Unpublished letter, April 7, 1924. In Scribner Archive, Princeton University Library, Princeton, N.J.

———. In *Dear Scott/Dear Max: The Fitzgerald-Perkins Correspondence.* Edited by John Kuehl and Jackson Bryer. New York: Scribner, 1971.

———. Letters to Hemingway and Elizabeth Lemmon. In *Max Perkins: Editor of Genius* by A. Scott Berg. New York: Riverhead Books, 1997.

Piper, Henry Dan, comp. *Fitzgerald's The Great Gatsby: The Novel, the Critics, the Background.* New York: Scribner, 1970.

Pound, Ezra. *The Letters of Ezra Pound, 1907–1941.* Edited by D. D. Paige. New York: Haskell House, 1974.

Richardson, Brian. *Print Culture in Renaissance Italy: The Editor and the Vernacular Text, 1470–1600.* Cambridge: Cambridge University Press, 2004.

Sante, Luc. *The Factory of Facts.* New York: Pantheon, 1998.

———. *Low Life: Lures and Snares of Old New York.* New York: Farrar, Straus and Giroux, 2003.

Sebald, W. G. *The Rings of Saturn.* Translated by Michael Hulse. New York: New Directions, 1999.

Seldes, Gilbert. "New York Chronicle." *The New Criterion* (London) 4, June 1926.

Smart, Elizabeth. *By Grand Central Station I Sat Down and Wept; and The Assumption of the Rogues & Rascals.* New York: Vintage, 1992.

Spencer, Scott. *A Ship Made of Paper*. New York: HarperCollins, 2003.

Strunk, William, Jr. *The Elements of Style*. With revisions, an introduction, and a chapter on writing by E. B. White. New York: Macmillan, 1979.

Thomas, Rosanne Daryl. *The Angel Carver*. New York: Random House, 1995.

Thompson, Jim. *Pop. 1280*. New York: Vintage, 1990.

Thorpe, Adam. *Ulverton*. London: Secker & Warburg, 1992.

Thorpe, James. "The Aesthetics of Textual Criticism." *PMLA* vol. 80, no. 5 (December 1965): 465–82. (On censorship in the eighteenth, nineteenth, and twentieth centuries.)

Thurman, Judith. *Secrets of the Flesh: A Life of Colette*. New York: Knopf, 1999.

Wakefield, Neville. Afterword. In *'71-NY* by Daido Moriyama and Neville Wakefield. New York: PPP in association with Roth Horowitz, 2002.

Weinberger, Eliot. "What I Heard About Iraq." In *What Happened Here: Bush Chronicles*. New York: New Directions, 2005.

Wrede, Stuart. *Kaj Franck: Designer*. Porvoo-Helsinki-Juva: Museum of Applied Arts, 1992.

Yagoda, Ben. *About Town:* The New Yorker *and the World It Made*. New York: De Capo Press, 2001. (Contains quotes by John Cheever, Ved Mehta, Vladimir Nabokov, J. D. Salinger, and Kenneth Tynan.)

INTERVIEWS

Berger, Maurice. Interview with author. New York, summer 2003.

Botsford, Gardner. Interview with author. New York, winter 2004.

Caponegro, Mary. Interview with author. Rhinebeck, N.Y., summer 2003.

Epstein, Mitch. Interview with author. New York, winter 2004.

Franzen, Jonathan. Interview with author by correspondence. Fall 2003.

Freeman, Judith. Interview with author. New York, fall 2003.

Galassi, Jonathan. Interview with author. New York, winter 2002.

Bibliography

Gottlieb, Eli. Interview with author. New York, summer 2002.

Howard, Gerald. Interview with author. New York, fall 2001.

Kidder, Tracy. Interview with author by correspondence. Spring 2006.

Kipnis, Laura. Interview with author. New York, summer 2003.

Lewis, Jim. Interview with author. New York, summer 2002.

Mathews, Harry. Interview with author by correspondence. Winter 2003.

McDonough, Tom. Interview with author. New York, spring 2004.

Mobilio, Albert. Interview with author by correspondence. Fall 2004.

Morrow, Bradford. Interview with author by correspondence. Fall 2005.

Naddaff, Ramona. Interview with author by correspondence. Fall 2004.

Ondaatje, Michael. Interview with author by telephone. Spring 2006.

Patchett, Ann. Interview with author by telephone. Spring 2006.

Robertson, Robin. Interview with author by correspondence. Fall 2003.

Sante, Luc. Interview with author by correspondence. Spring 2004.

Spencer, Scott. Interview with author. Rhinebeck, N.Y., summer 2003.

Stone, D. S. Interview with author. New York, spring 2003.

Thorpe, Adam. Interview with author by correspondence. Summer 2003.

Weinberger, Eliot. Interview with author. New York, winter 2003.

Williams, Treat. Interview with author. New York, summer 2002.

ACKNOWLEDGMENTS

Many of the ideas in this book have been tried and tweaked in the course I teach at the New School Graduate Writing Program in New York. Thanks to Director Robert Polito for his commitment to my course on self-editing as a part of the curriculum. He runs his program with intellectual rigor and creativity that make teaching there a joy. Thanks to the program's Associate Director, Jackson Taylor, for his wise counsel, and to my students for their spirited investigations into editing.

To Eli Gottlieb, Jim Lewis, and Jeanne McCulloch for their excellent comments on the draft at different stages and their unflinching support; to Judy Clain and Dani Shapiro for their enthusiasm and efforts on my behalf.

Thanks to my editor, Jill Bialosky, and her associate, Evan Carver, for their critical guidance with tightening the manuscript, and to copy editor Elizabeth Pierson for her fastidious corrections.

Although more interviews were done than could be included, every one of them influenced this book. Profound thanks to the interviewees listed in the bibliography, as well as Roger Angell, Trisha Brown, Eric Fischl, April Gornick, Bruce Handy, David

Schwab, and Jack Stephens, for being generous with their time and thoughts. A special thanks to Adam Thorpe and Robin Robertson for giving readers the privilege of watching them work together.

To my agent, Sarah Burnes, for her editorial prowess and for encouraging me to write the book I wanted, not the one I thought I should.

My appreciation to Anita Naegeli for her tireless research assistance; Joel Kaye for his library tour and tips; Peter Freeman and Elisabeth Cunnick for a fine place to write; Andrew Roth for the ongoing, provocative conversation we have about editing; Laurie Wilson, who skillfully and kindly got me going; Hélène Leneveu, whose integrity as a childcare giver and friend made it easier for me to concentrate; and Christoph Gielen for his fiery faith in *The Artful Edit* and in me.

Thanks to the New York Public Library for giving me umbrage at the Wertheim and Allen Rooms.

Rob Spillman and Lee Montgomery at *Tin House* magazine published "Revisioning *The Great Gatsby*" and invited me to teach at the Tin House Summer Writer's Workshop. They, with their colleague Meg Storey, have steadily cheered this book on, for which I am grateful.

To my mothers: Helen Sherman, for making me look up words in the dictionary from the time I could lift one; and Jacqueline Bell, for taking my notebooks seriously. Their unconditional support kept the motor running even when the driver would disappear.

I am grateful to my husband, Mitch Epstein, for his example of persistence and independence of mind. Our professional collaborations on exhibitions and books have been a rich testing ground for my ideas on editing. Mitch's patience, loyalty, and sharp advice have been indispensable.

Deepest thanks to my daughter, Lucia Bell-Epstein, for accepting that writing and mothering can go together, though not always comfortably. Her respect for my work and love of language helped fuel this project.

CREDITS

Credits